C000217431

Vision On

5

FOREWORD

I first met Sean Ellis on a fashion shoot and immediately felt at home with his own contagious brand of wry British humour. He has the kind of edgy and irreverent eye I admire, never taking himself too seriously, always quitely and politely questioning his world with a refreshing and quirky talent.

365-A Year in Fashion is all about the spontaneous and sociological art of photojournalism and chronicles every single day in the fashion photographer's year. And not just any old year: 1999, the last year of the millennium.

Sean's world is the world of the wanderer, carefully captured in a small room. No squinting, no cheating, no caricatures. Always candid and even innocent. But every artist is driven by obsession. Famous for his off-beat portraits of some of the most profilic celebrities of our generation, and his darkly obsessive and sexually aggressive flashes of fashion aesthetics, this time Sean clicks onto the lighter side of obsession with "downtime" pictures relentlessly recorded in real time with those renowned images. Day-in, day-out, Sean leads us a merry chase from Paris to Thailand to New York. But this is not yet another AliceThrough the Looking Glass. Neither mystifying nor demystifying, he catches people off their guard, laying bare the ordinary things of life with snapshots of his own boy's and girl's club, the studio, behind-the-scenes vignettes, or private moments with Erin and Kubrick, his endearing if somewhat enigmatic canine companion.

Sean meticulously creates a valuable contemporary statement that visibly nourishes his own special contribution to fashion photography in a stream of images that grab you and stay with you like a snatch of music you can't get out of your head. Especially that groovy hound dog Kubrick!

John Galliano

INTRODUCTION

Imagine doing a picture every day for a whole year? The idea captivated me immediately. What suddenly became apparent is that your life can be very monotonous and boring. The idea compelled me to try new things, travel to new places and meet new people. In fact, the idea made my life move forward at great speed as I leapt into the unknown in search of an interesting moment to represent that particular day. It is an attitude that I try and live by even though the project is finished.

The camera for me is a time machine. It is able to stop time and allows the viewer to visually re-enter into that frozen moment. The project re-kindled my interest into the dynamics of photography, not just to take pictures commercially but to take pictures for the love of taking pictures.

The project was a huge undertaking. At the end of 1999, we had around 2000 contact sheets which adds up to around 50,000 pictures. Some days had only one picture while other days had two hundred pictures. The printing and editing process took a further year before we started on the design. During this period the book hit all sorts of problems from personal to professional to financial and was "off" then "on" more times than I can count. You read this only because of the hard work and determination of a few people who stayed true to their word.

I look back on the photographs now and I see faces filled with hopes and dreams, laughter and love and I'm reminded of something that was once said to me. A photograph of you smiling at the camera is a postcard sent from you in the present to you in the future and it says "you were having a good time."

Sean Ellis, June 2002

1

The first day of the year, Val D'Isere, France

02 Val D'Isere
03-03a Self timer portraits of Jason and me reading
04 Me snowboarding
05 Dog in winter coat

4
5
2

9

06 Jason with the giggles
07 Filming snowboarding on Super 8
08 Jason and me partied out, Val D'Isere
09 Arrive home late and find Kayte asleep in my flat
10 Postproduction, Jean Paul Gaultier commercial, Glassworks, London

BLOW
JOB
PILLS

11

Printing of Isabella Blow's Birthday Party. Clockwise from top left; Alexander McQueen and Issy Blow; Lucy Ferry; L–R, Sophie Dahl, friend, Jeremy Scott and Danilo Milic; Alexander McQueen; Tim Noble and Sue Webster

12

Printing session of Gisele for *Big* magazine, London

16

17

13

14

13 Helen Stinton on a go-see, London
14 Gallery window, London
15 One day meeting with Nadja Auermann, Monaco
16 Kubrick proving it's a dogs life, London
17 Isabella and Detmar have Sunday lunch, Live Bait, London

15

18

20

21

23

22 Lara Belmont for *The Sunday Times*, London
23 Location hunting in Gloucestershire

Helen Stinton for *The Face*, Gloucestershire

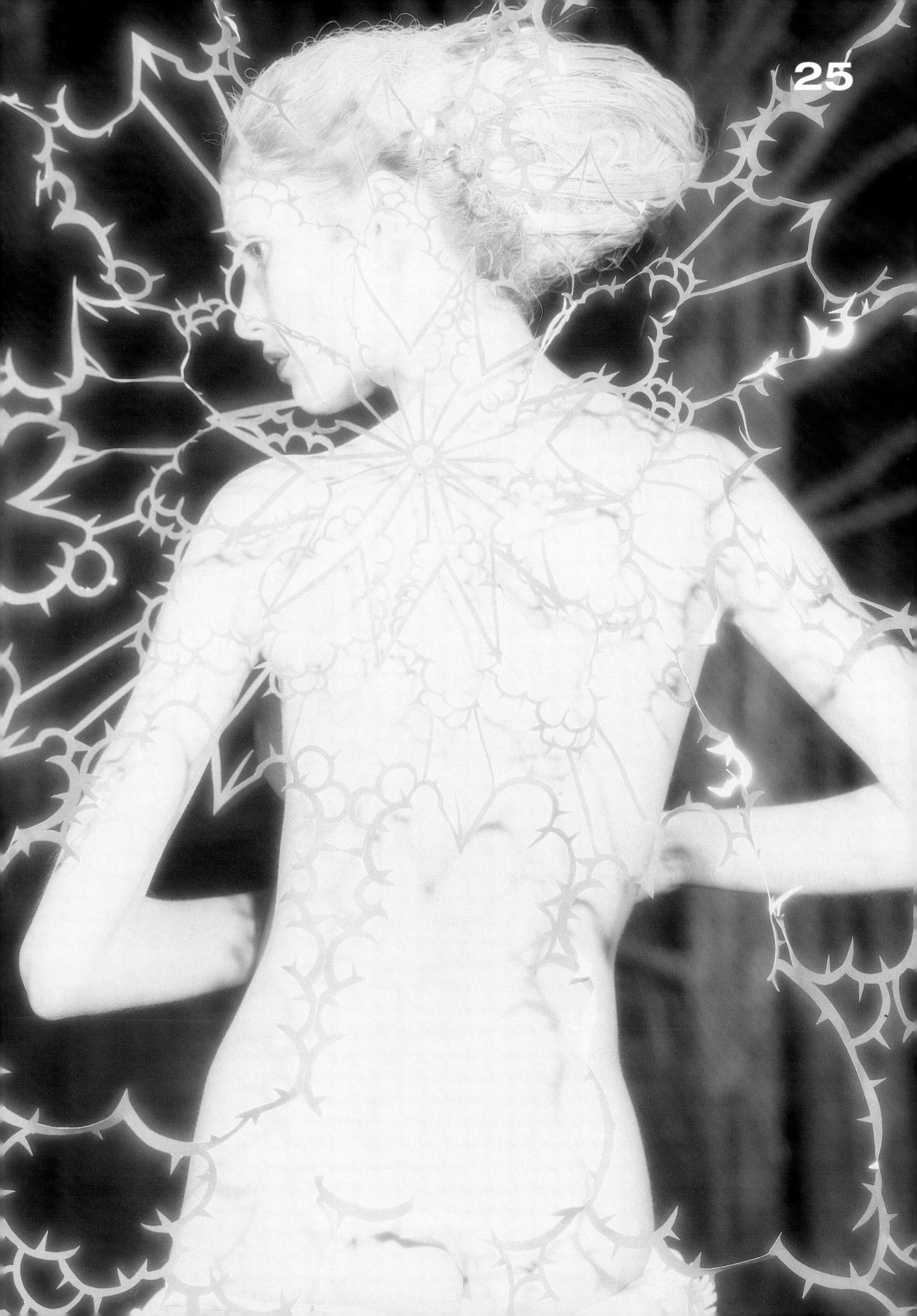

26 Fly to Mexico **27** Kiko dives into a Cenote
28 5.45am **28a** Gio and I go location hunting **28b** Scott, Neil and Eli scream at the sea, Tulum, Mexico

28a 28b

29–31 Gisele for *The Face*, Tulum, Mexico

29

30

31

31b Gisele helps to fill the camera hole

32 Scott and Gisele, Tulum, Mexico
32a Behind the scenes

32

33

Gisele, Scott and I battle with wind, sunburn and 10x8 cameras

34 35 34a

34 Neil, Gio and Catherine hold on for dear life on the back of our Beetle cabriolet
34a A Mexican solider patrols the beach
35 Arrive in New York
36–36a Joy for *Visionaire*

36

36a

37–37a Mini Anden and Yfke Sturm on a go-see **38–38b** Audrey Marni, New York **39** Erin has a pre birthday night on the tiles; Bay and Erin in a cab, New York **40** Uptown, New York City

USA TODAY
CHANEL
BUSES ONLY
DON'T BLOCK THE BOX
CHASE
CHASE
CHASE
38
38a
38b
39
40

41
42
42a
Acer
Computers & Peripherals
Welcome to
NEW YORK

45

41–42a Liberty and I spend 14 hours in JFK airport during a pilot strike
43 Meeting with my lawyers Esther Mallach and Detmar Blow
44 Kubrick and me
45 Kayte and Gio leave me a polaroid
46 Printing the Mexico story with Brian Dowling

Natasha in Veronique Branquinho for *i-D* magazine

48 50

48 Kubrick on the heath
49 Curtain road, London
50 Sierra on a go-see
51–52 Brett Anderson for *The Face*

49

51

52

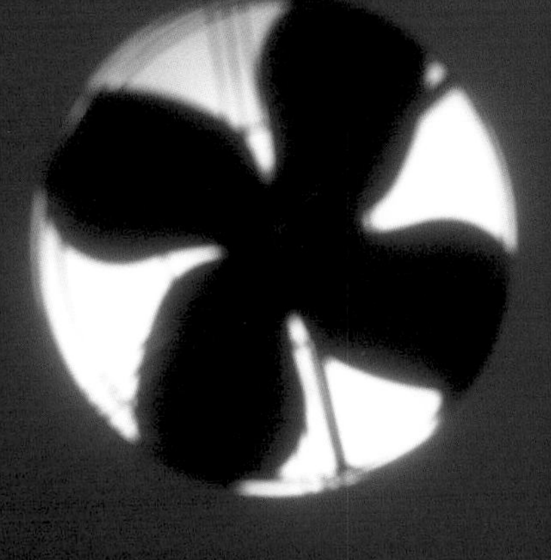

Clockwise from top left; Stella McCartney and Plum Sykes; Amber Valetta; Michael Roberts and Anna Wintour; John Galliano and Isabella Blow all at the *Vogue* party, Christies, London

Anna Wintour and Hamish Bowles at Alexander McQueen's 'Overlook' show

54

55

55 "My favourite pictures of your's were the 'up the skirt' ones" Kylie
55a Patrick Cox and Kylie Minogue, *Visionaire* party, Harvey Nichols, London.

57

56 *Arena Homme Plus*, London
57 Hank taking a break during post production on *Arena*, Illusions, London
58 Strip joint
59 The family portrait

59

58

60

64

Previous page: **60** Reprinting of Audrey for *American Vogue*, originally shot in NY 1998 and printed in London
This spread: **61** Portrait of me by Gio
62 Kayte, Gio, Kubrick and me, the office, London
63 Matt and Emma snogging, pool rooms, Hackney
64 Council estate for Kelly Klein's book 'Crosses', London

65

66

67

68

70

65 Kubrick jumping fences in Victoria Park, London
66 Fashion feet, Paris
67 Brian and me colour printing
68 Long distance phone call
69 Givenchy runway show, Paris
70 Audrey and Maggie backstage at Galliano, Paris
71 Japanese school girls

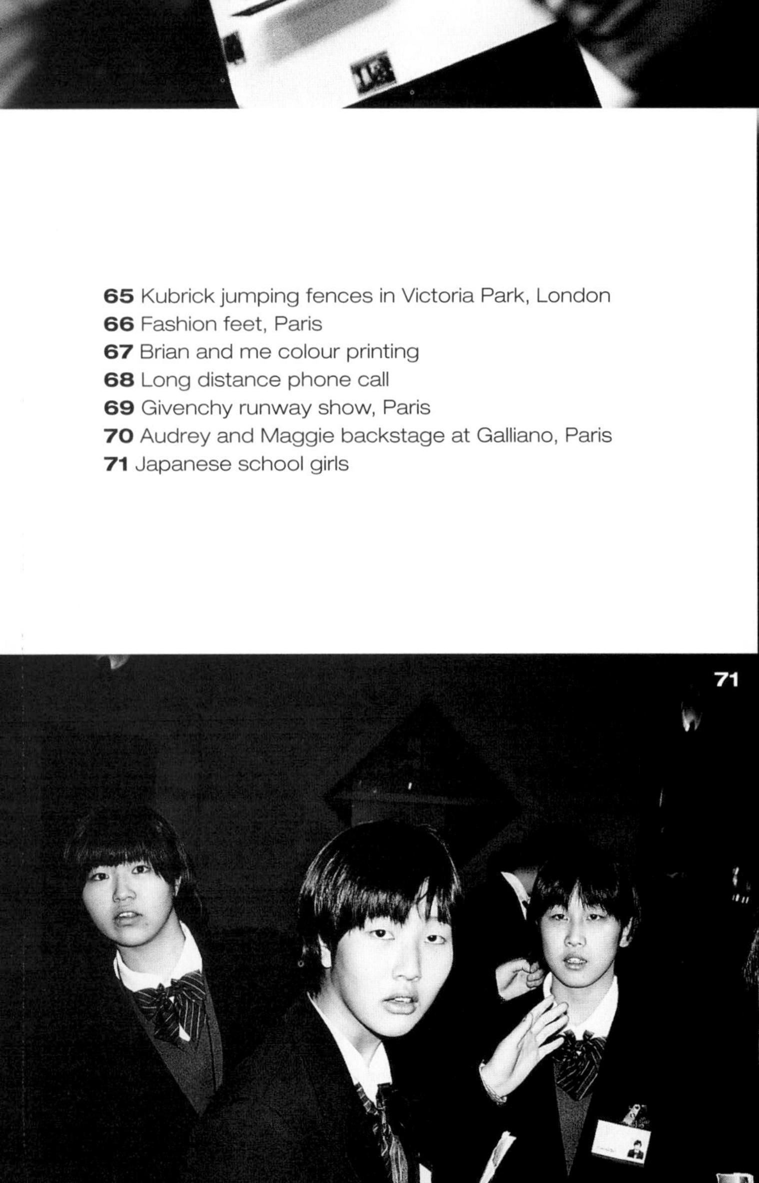

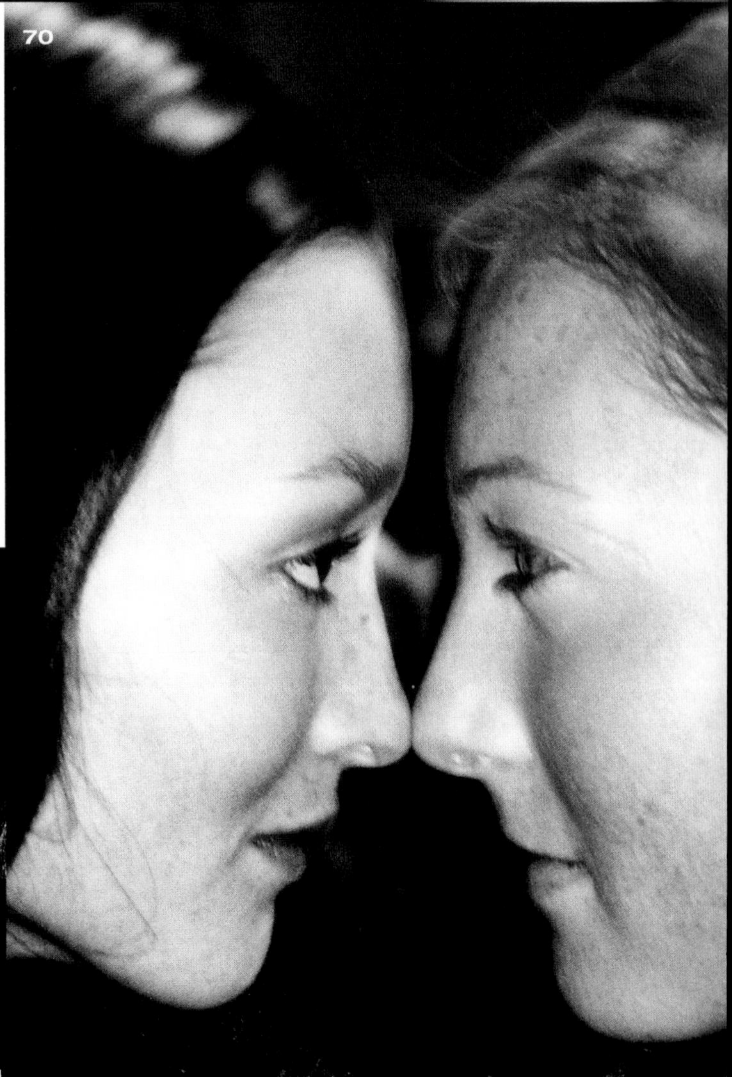

71

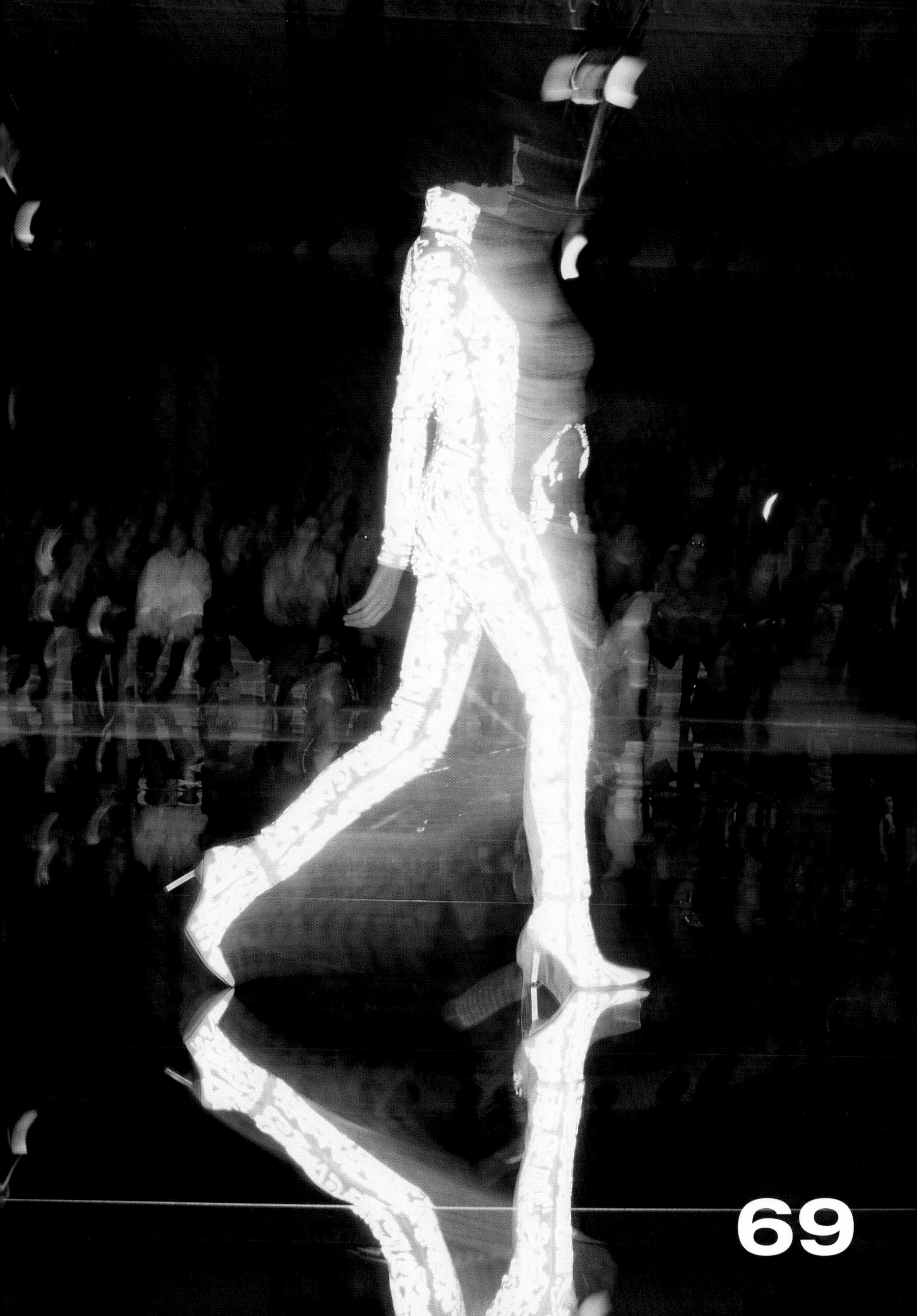
69

Jade Parfit for *The New York Times*, Paris

74

The Devil for *Visionaire*

75 Erin and I take the Eurostar back to London to catch a plane to New York
76 Arrive in New York for a pre-light
77 Lonneke for beauty campaign, New York

75 76

77

78

78 L-R, Me, James Kaliardos, Niki Taylor and Yamila Diaz discuss the beauty shot
79 Erin in her apartment
80 Kayte waiting for a taxi in Times Square, NY
81 New York from my hotel room
82 Erin at night

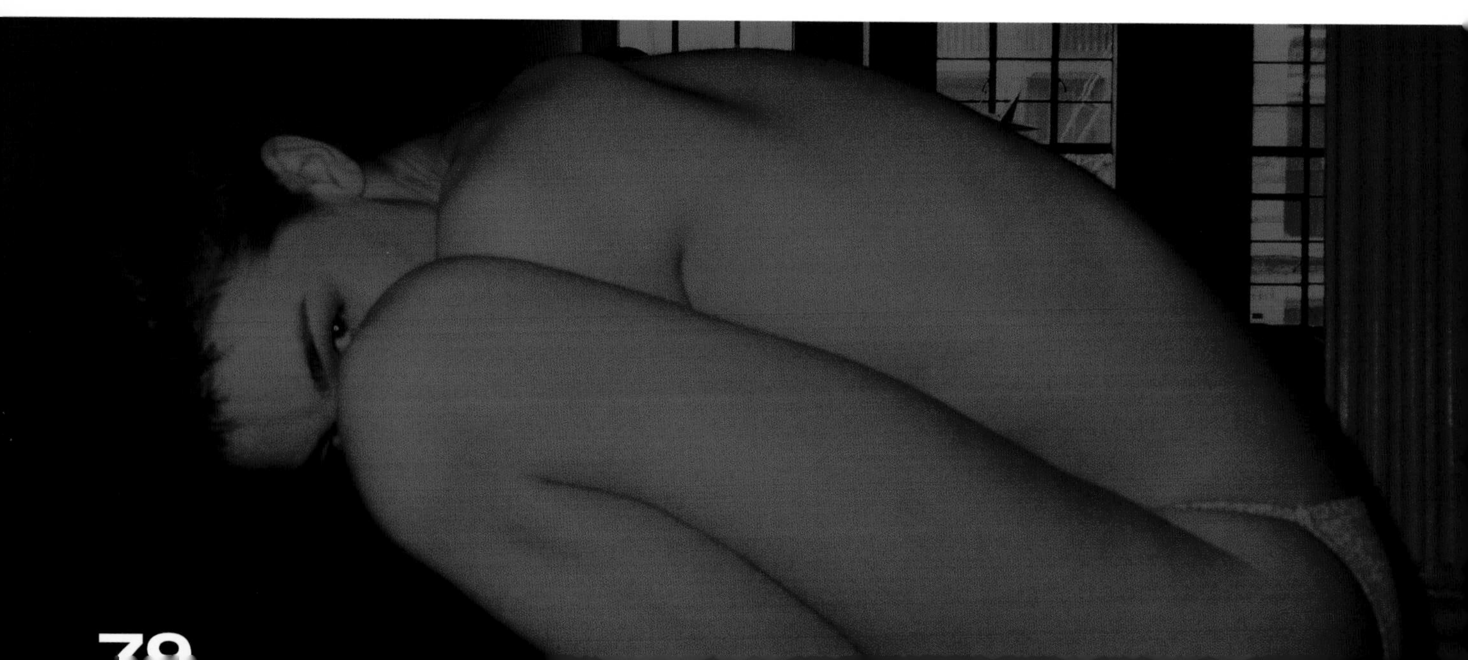

80

81

82

Erin asleep, Soho Grand, New York

83

84

85

86

87

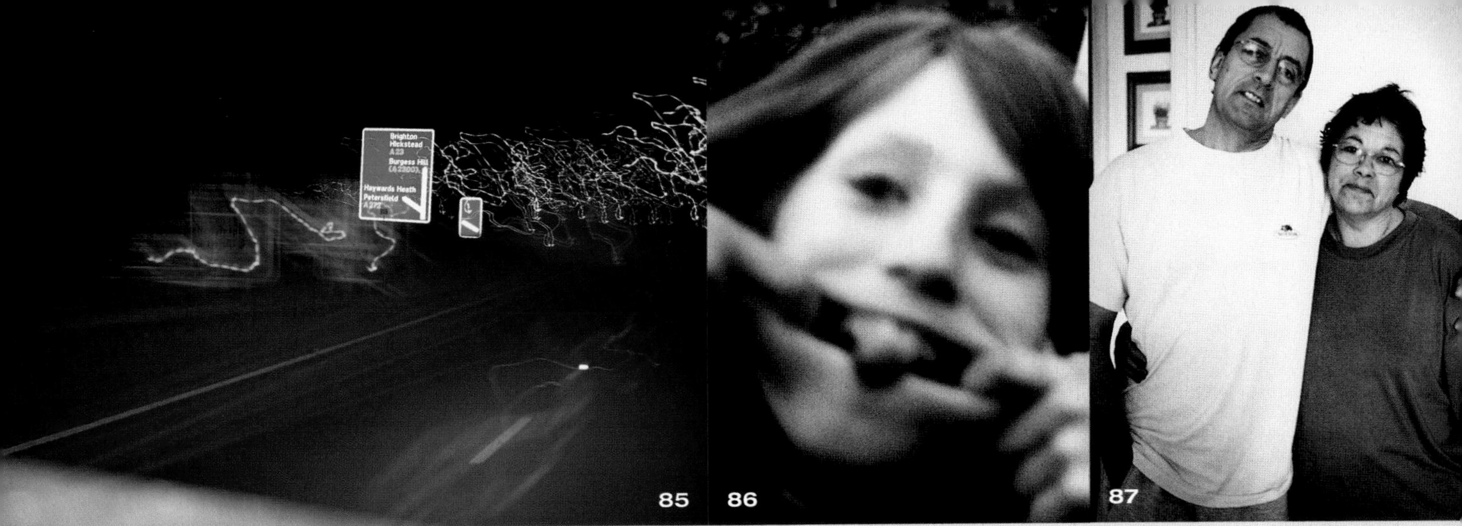

84 Fly back to London
85 Drive to Brighton
86 Kids, Brighton
87 Mum and Dad
88 Kubrick is happy that I'm home

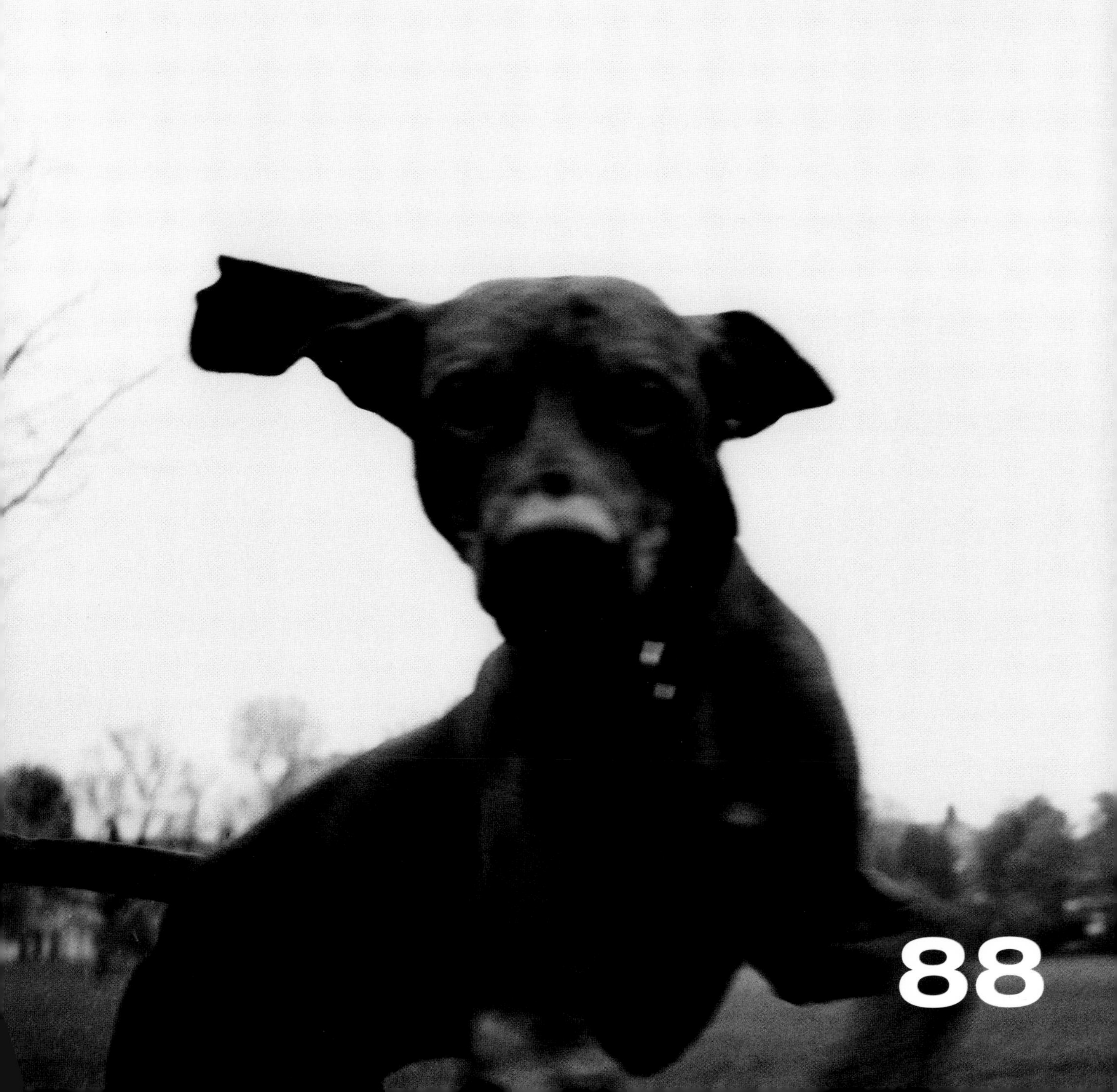

88

89 Nan

91 Drive back to London

94

95

95a

93 Kubrick, Victoria Park, London

Matt and Emma

96

Contact sheet of Erin and Kubrick

Erin watching T.V. **97**

Self portrait on the Eurostar **98**

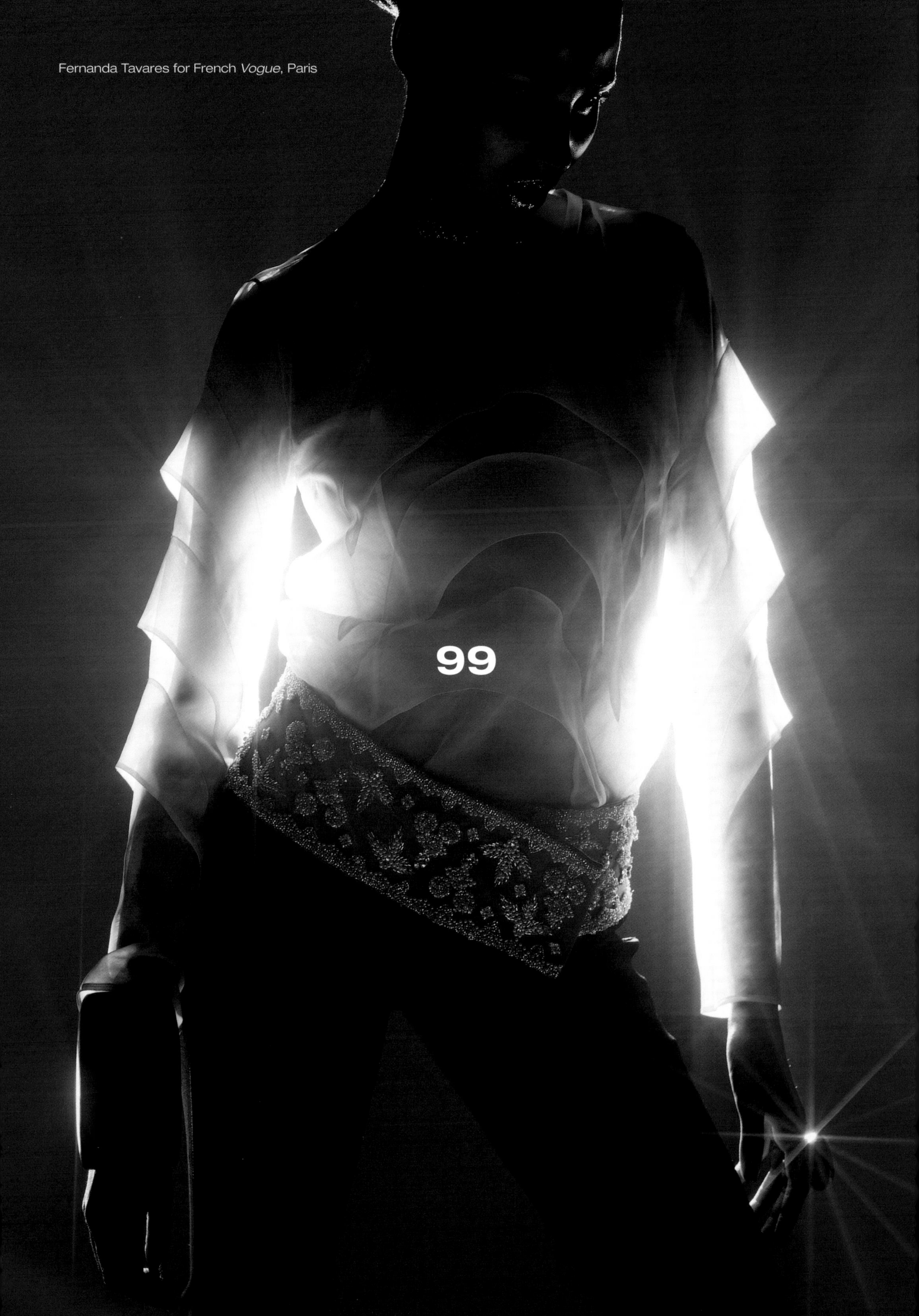

Fernanda Tavares for French *Vogue*, Paris

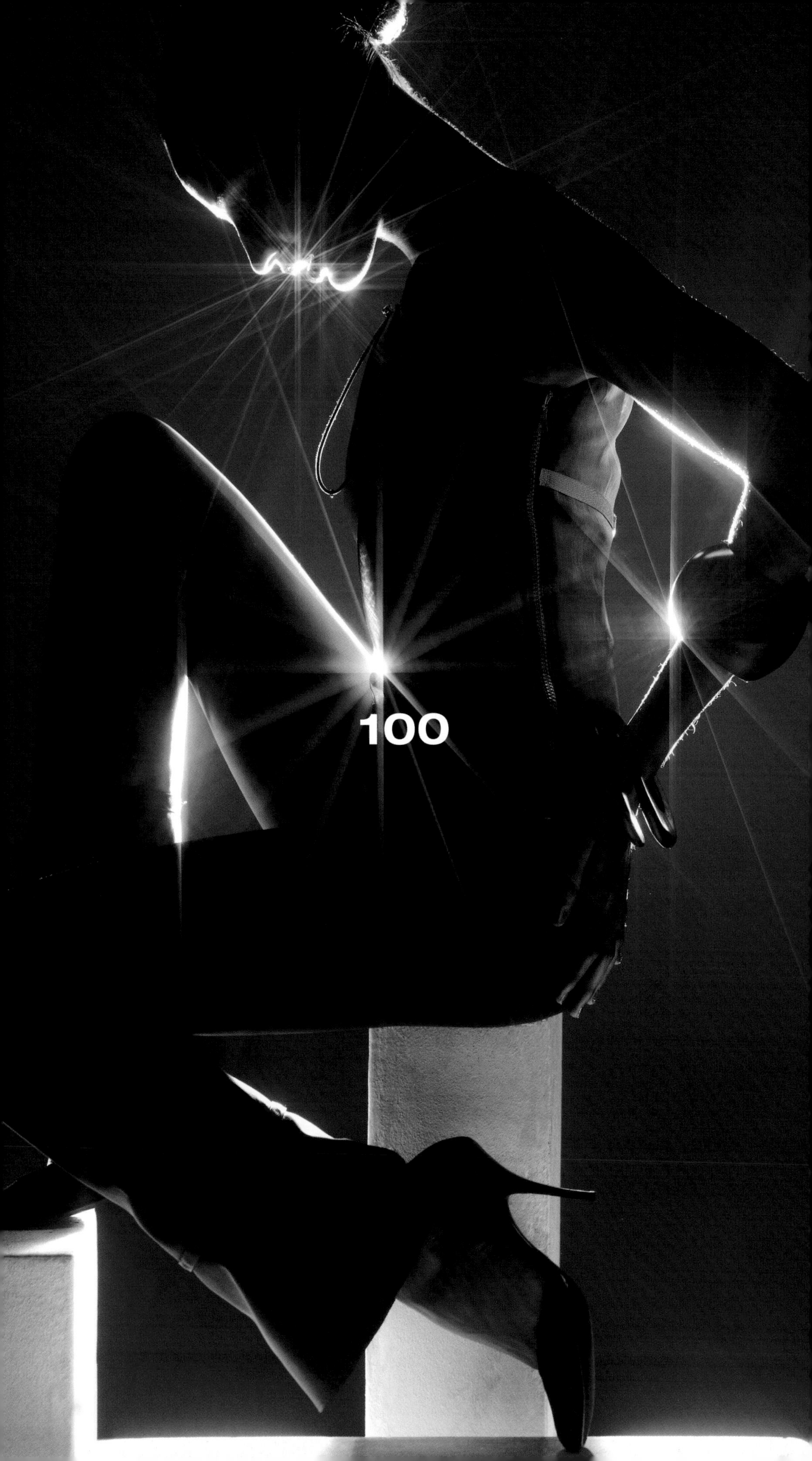
100

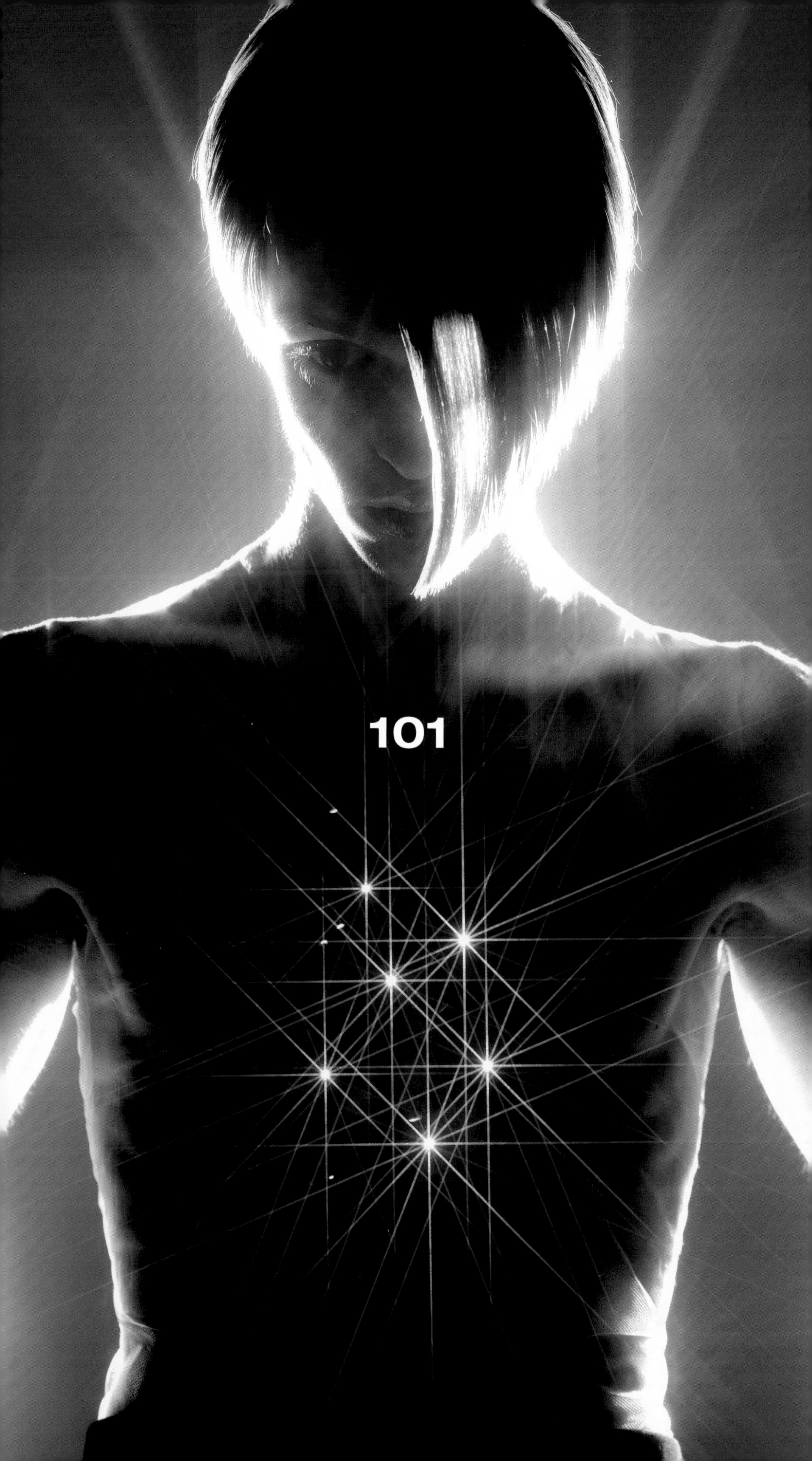
101

102

104

101 Yves Saint Laurent for *Visionaire*, Paris
102 Erin, Hotel Costes, Paris
103 Liz Collins and me, London
104 Man at a bus stop, London

103

105

Bryan Ferry

106 Stella McCartney

107 Jason Lodge and Carlo Brandelli

Press shoot for Carlo Brandelli, London

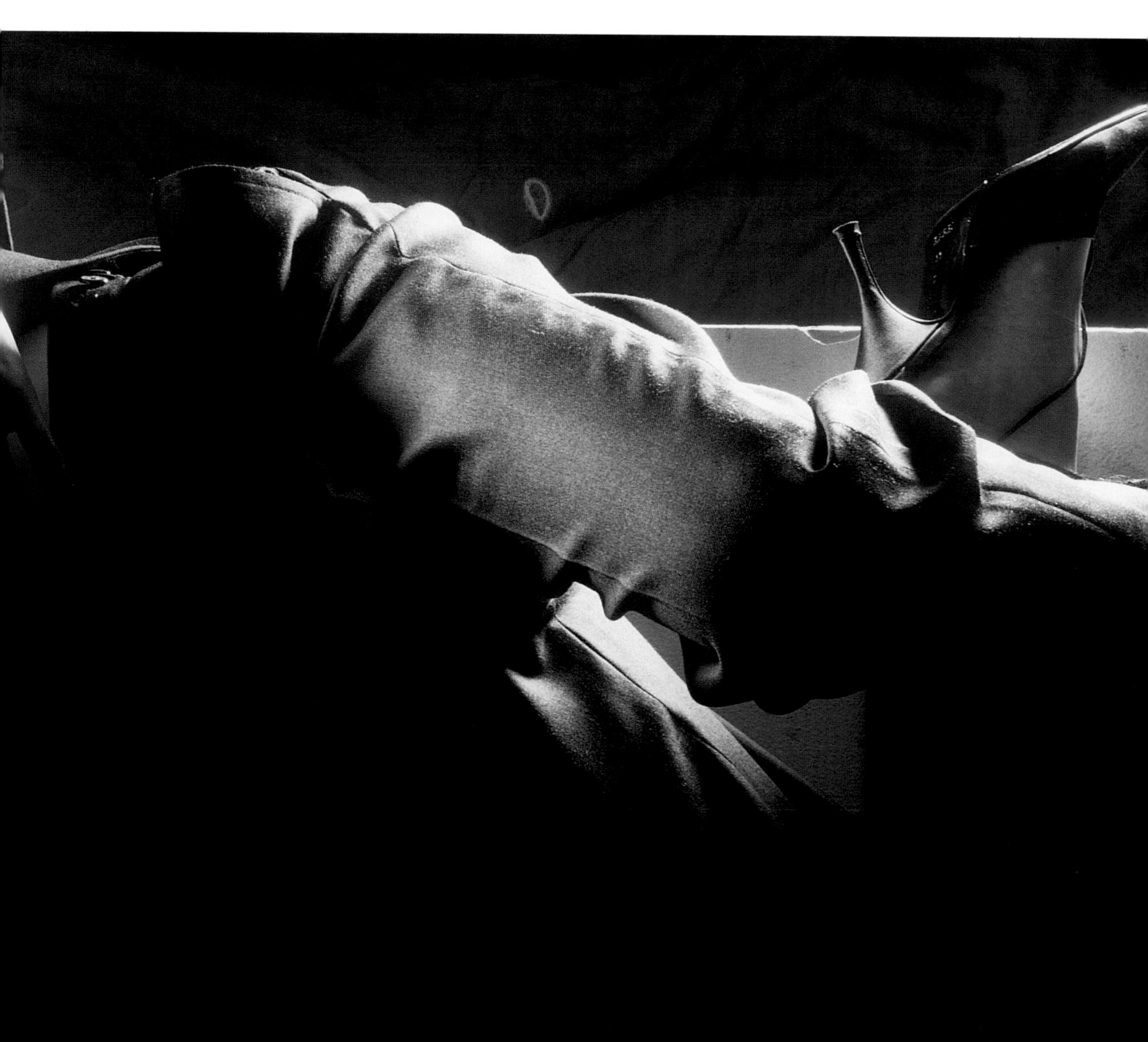

The Chemical Brothers for *i-D* magazine, London

111 Erin does a handstand on my desk

114 Karina Givargisoff's birthday party at the Kabaret club

114a Sharlene, Kayte and Erin, Kabaret

115 Reading in a café, Paris

116 Erin removes her make-up, Paris

112 Models party

113

113-113a Erin shopping in Harvey Nichols

114b Erin and me, Kabaret

114c Me and Matt, Kabaret

117 Kayte and Jeremy Scott, London

118 Matt poses for a pre-light, Patrick Cox, London

119

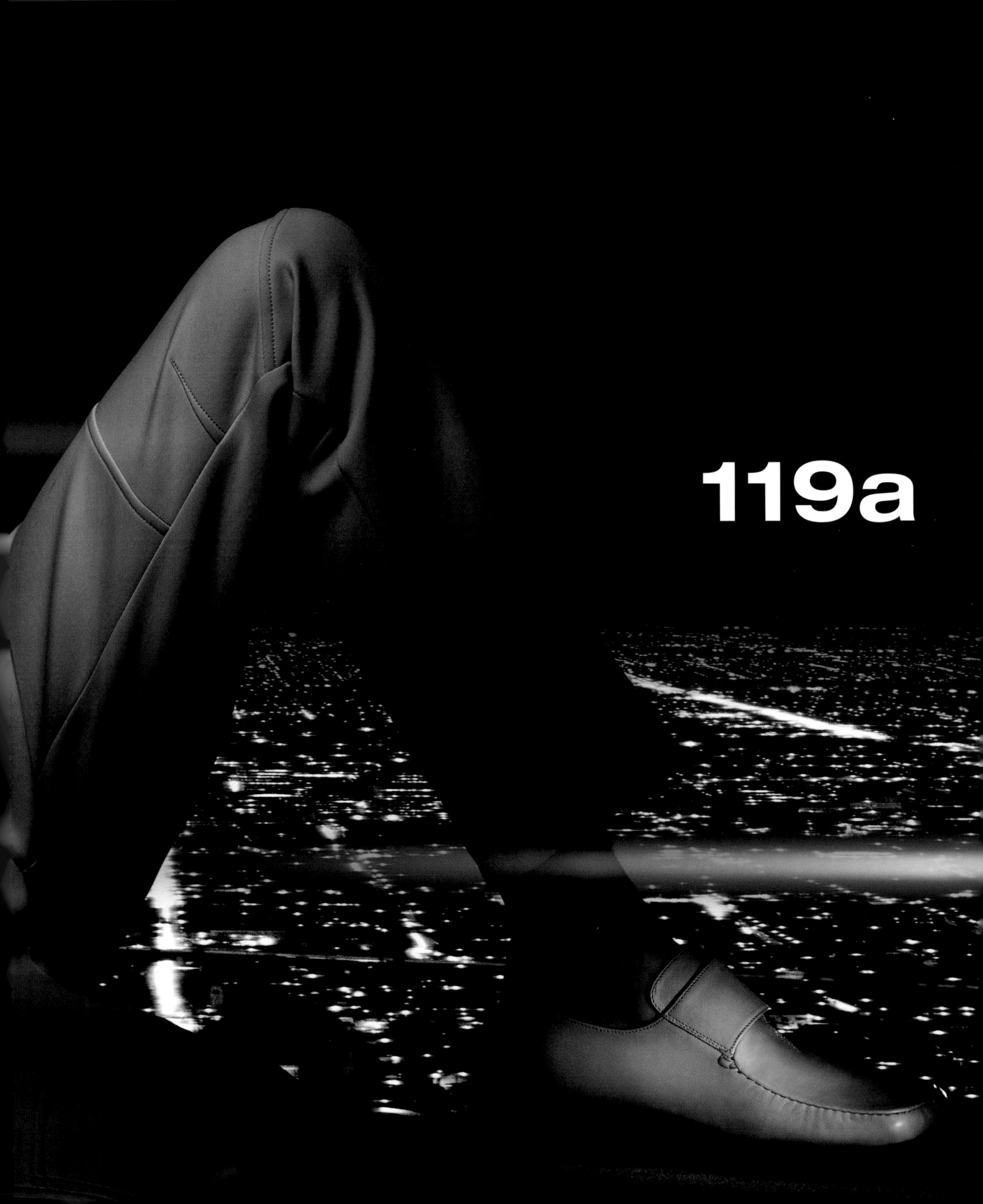

119a

The 'Gisele' issue of *Big* magazine have their launch party in the DKNY store, London
L–R Jason, me, Dad (hidden), Emma, Matt, Kayte and Erin

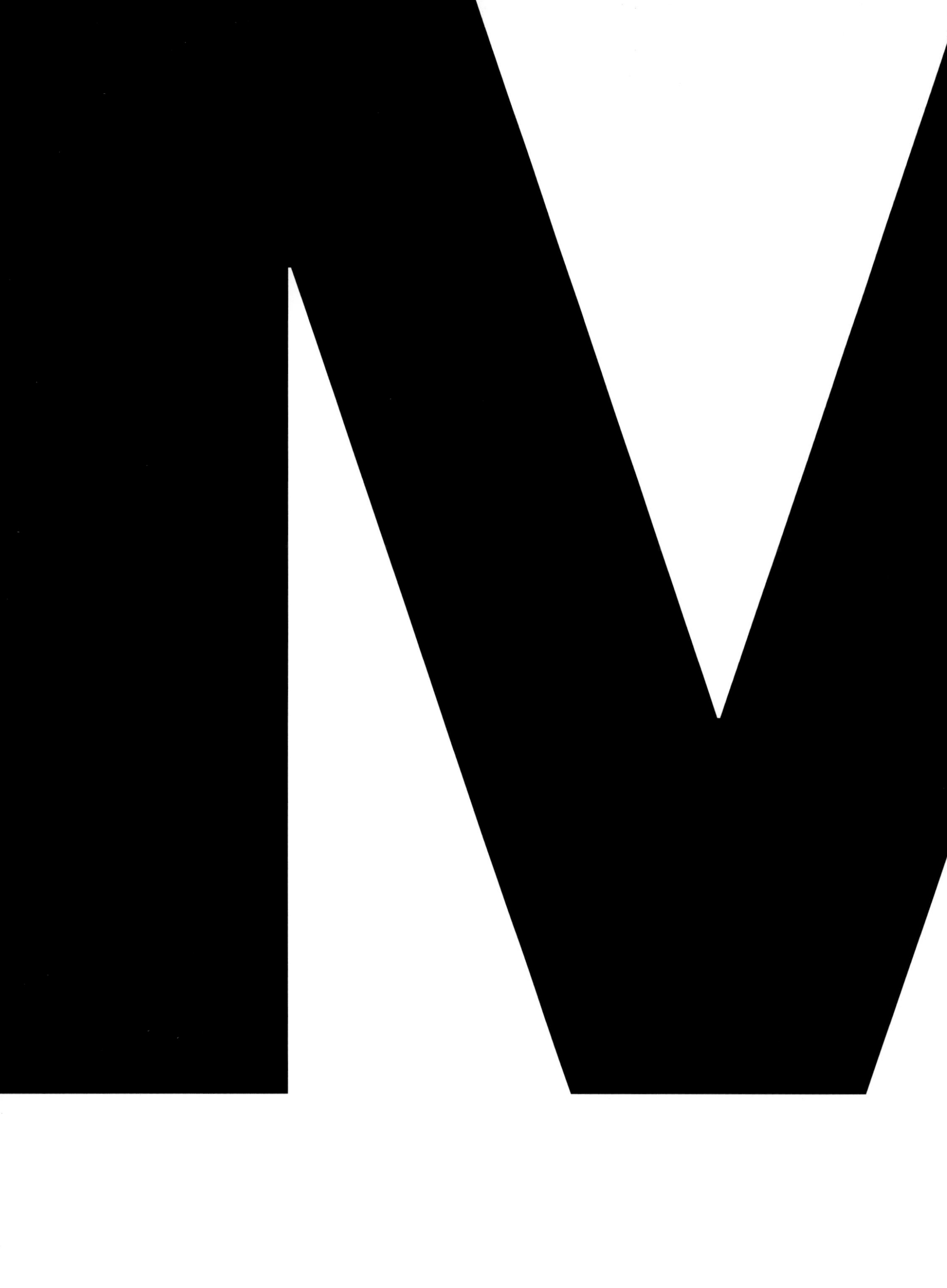

Kirsten Pieters for *Visionaire* magazine

122

124

123

125

126

126a

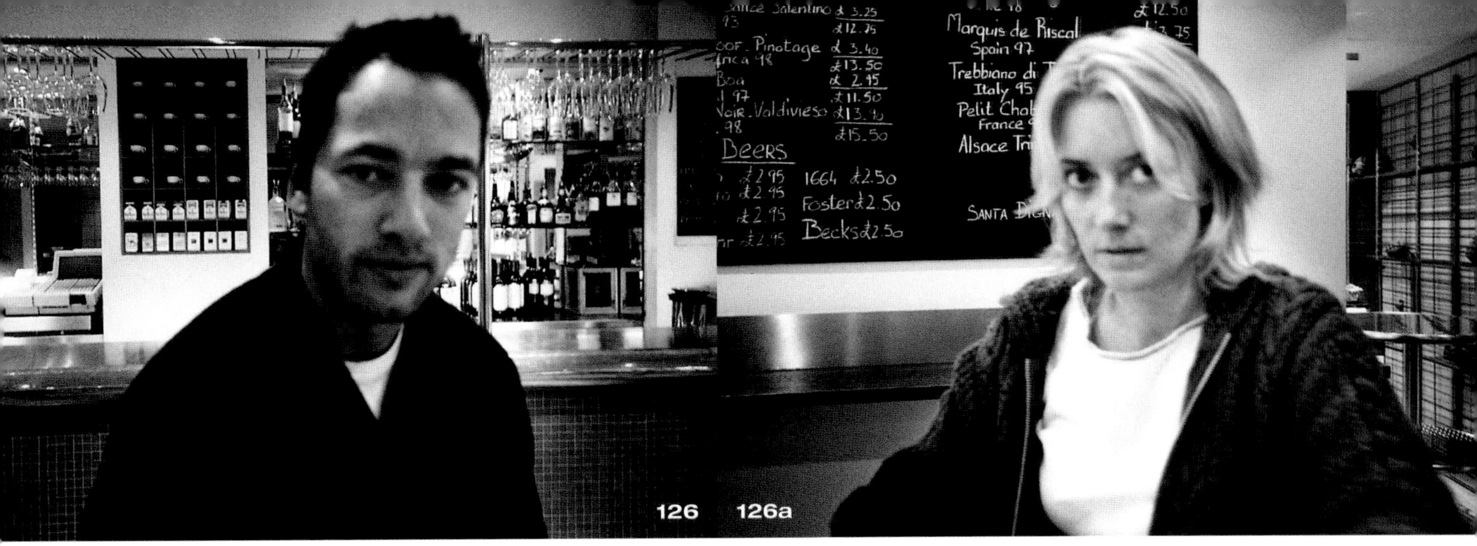

122 Carlo, Dad, Matt and Jason have a night out on the piss
123 Emma nurses Matt's hangover
124 Kubrick being Kubrick
125 The ongoing office gag
126 My film producer Lene Bausager takes a picture of me
126a I take a picture of Lene
127 Drive to Brighton

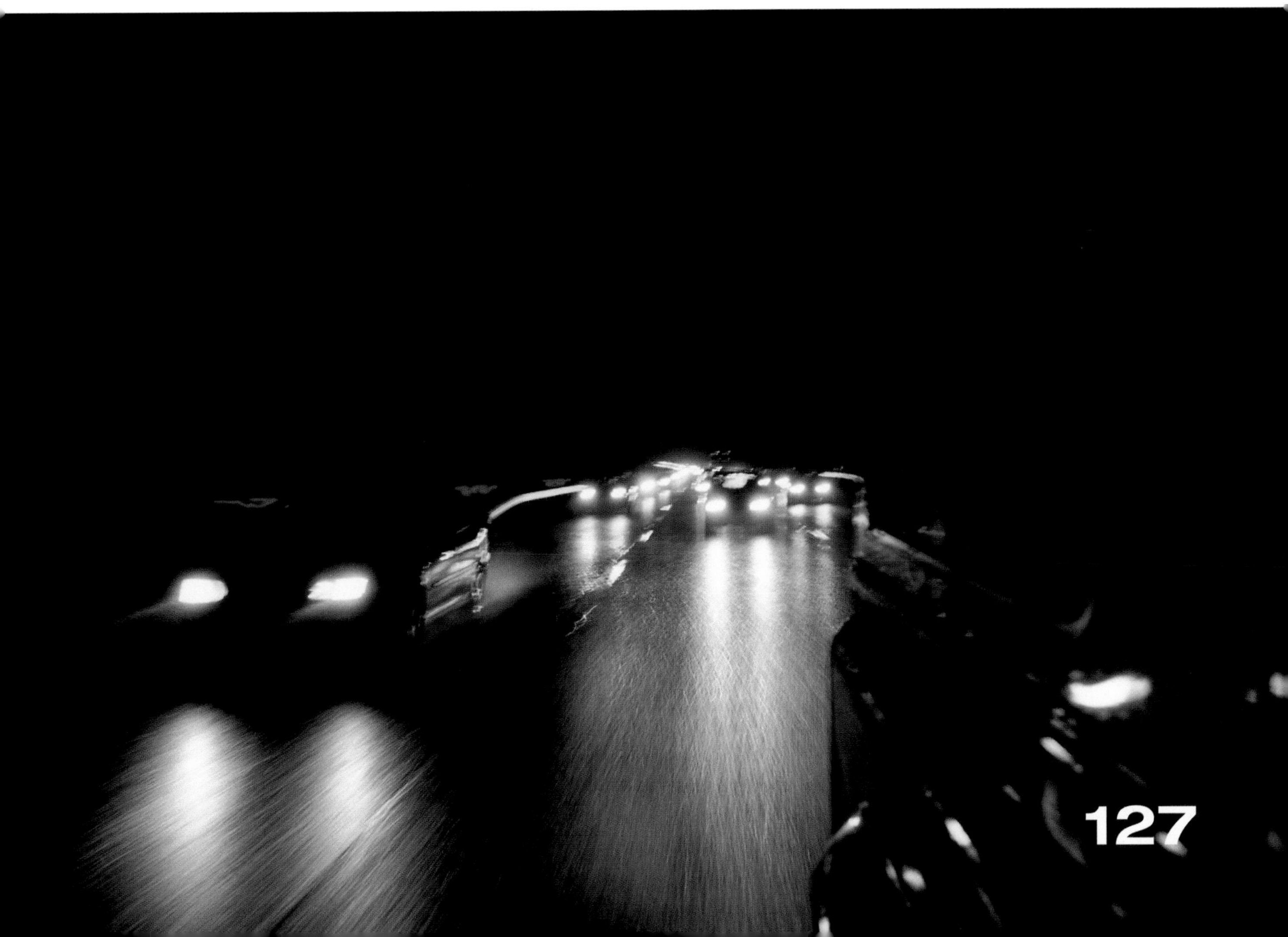

127

128 Filming of 'The Bill'

129 Erin asleep reflected in a T.V. screen

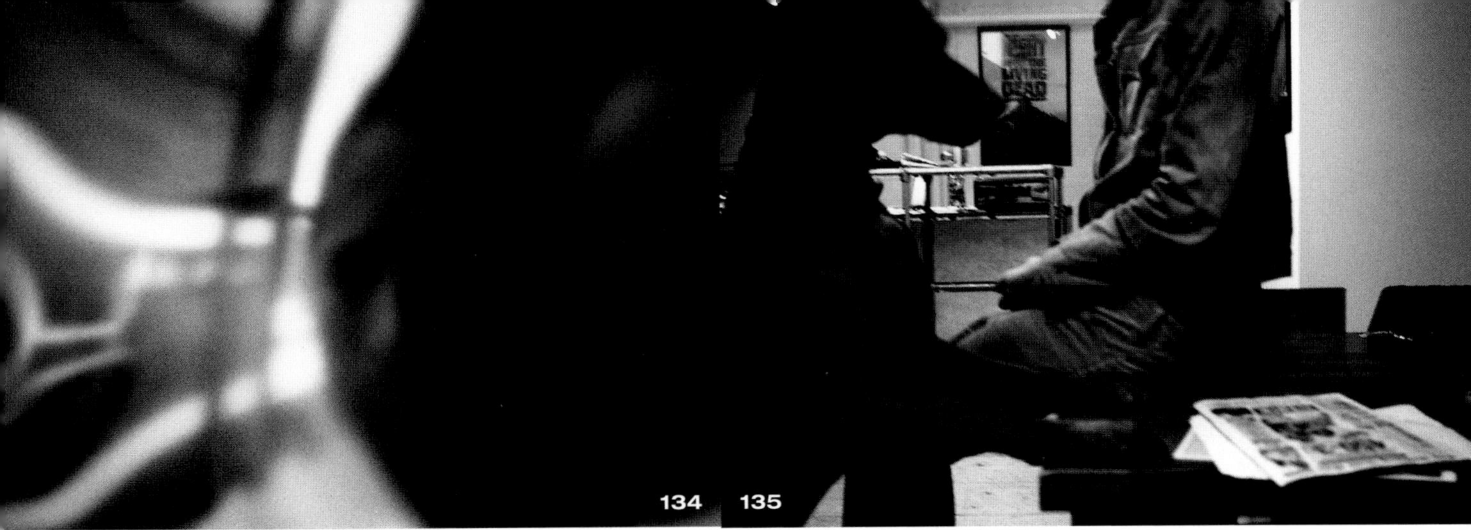

134 135

133

132 Erin
133 An office polaroid
134 Self portrait in a wine glass
135 Erin and Kubrick in the office
136-136c Erin and her nephew Ciaran play around in the garden, Birmingham

136  136a

136b  136c

137

Arrive in Paris for one night, self portrait

138

Film still from 'Lolita', my favourite film of the year.

139 The South Downs

140 Kubrick in an alley, Hackney, London

141

elga de Silva Blow Perera

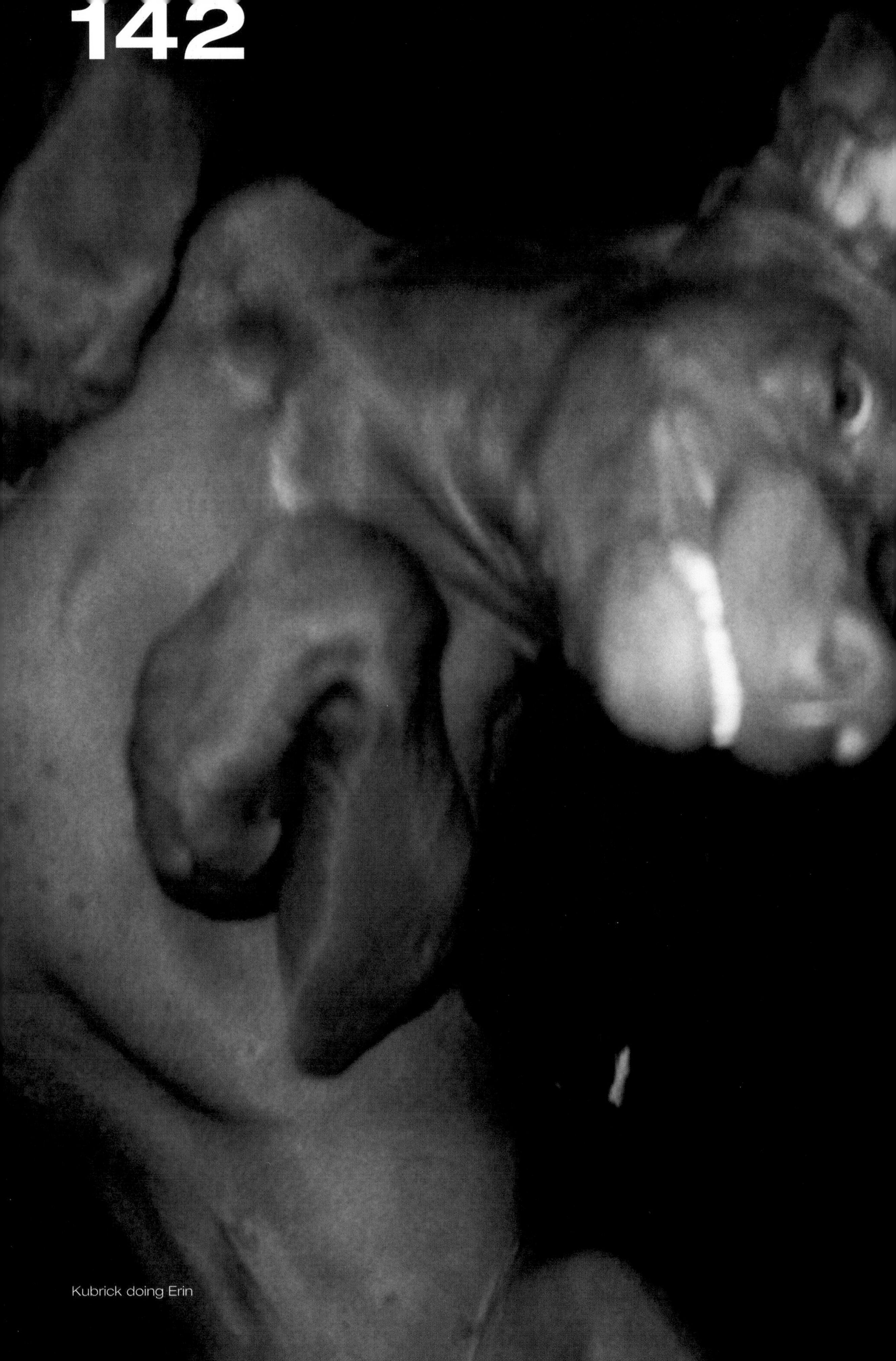

Kubrick doing Erin

Erin doing Kubrick

144

145

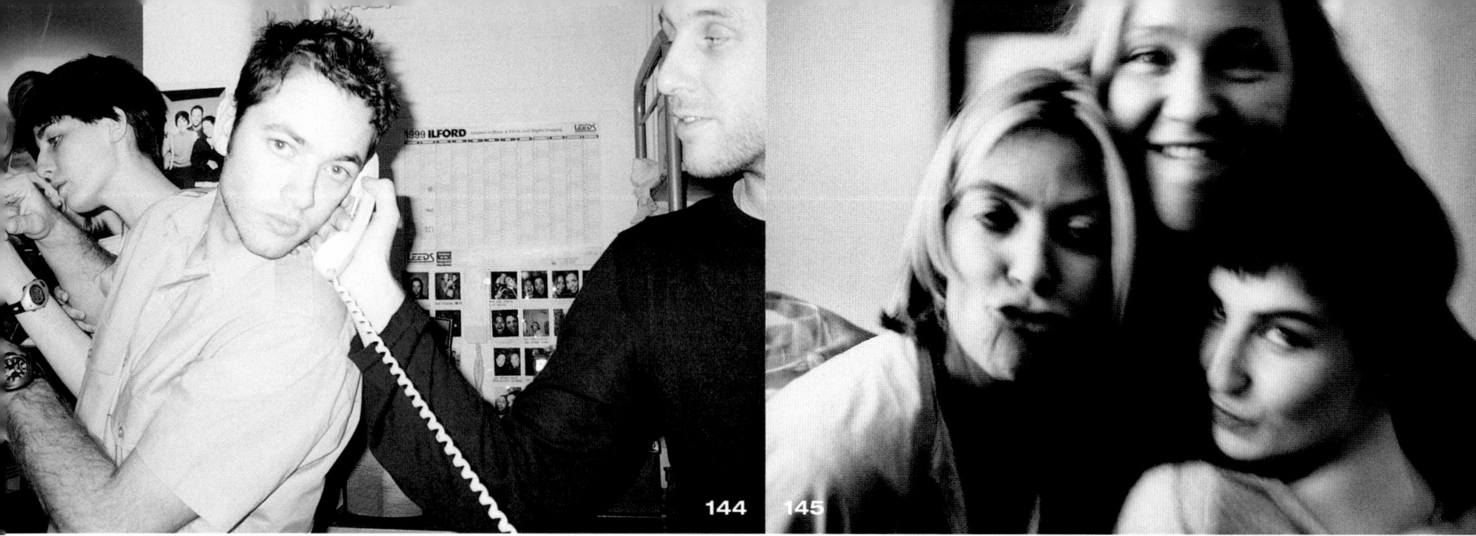

144 Erin, me and Matt in the office, London
145 Ellis, Tori, and Erin playing silly buggers, Metro Studios, London
146 Karen and Raphael, London
147 Erin with Kubrick, Victoria Park, London
148 Erin in the bath, my flat, London

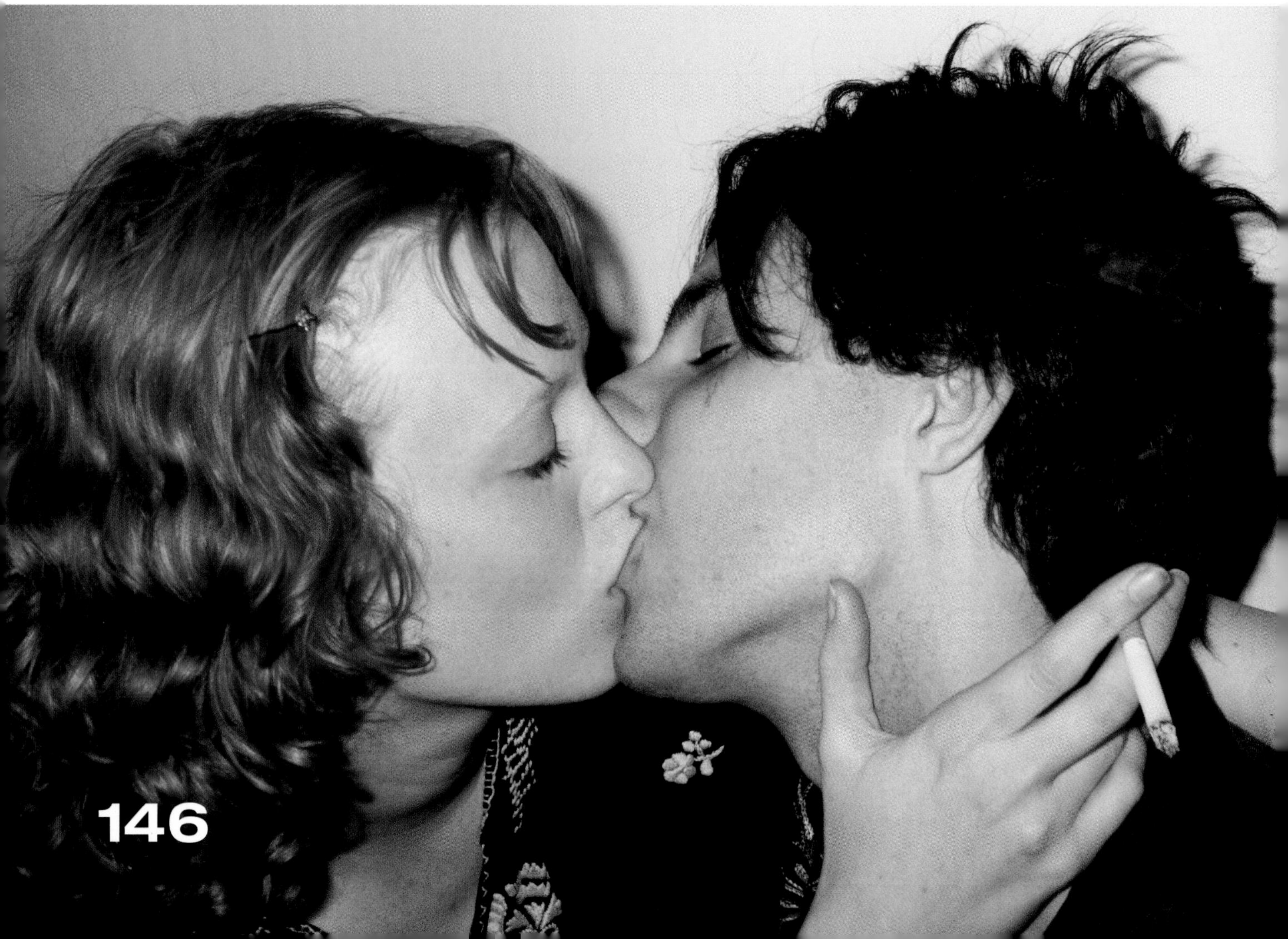
146

147

148

149

150

149 Kubrick and Alfie playing, the Bricklayers Arms, London
150 Kubrick on Brighton beach
151 Kubrick asleep on Erin driving back from Brighton.

151

152

152 Pre-light for Plein Sud campaign, Paris
153–154 Plein Sud campaign

153

153a

155 Matt is 'vexed', London
156 Jason in a club, London
157 Nude, London

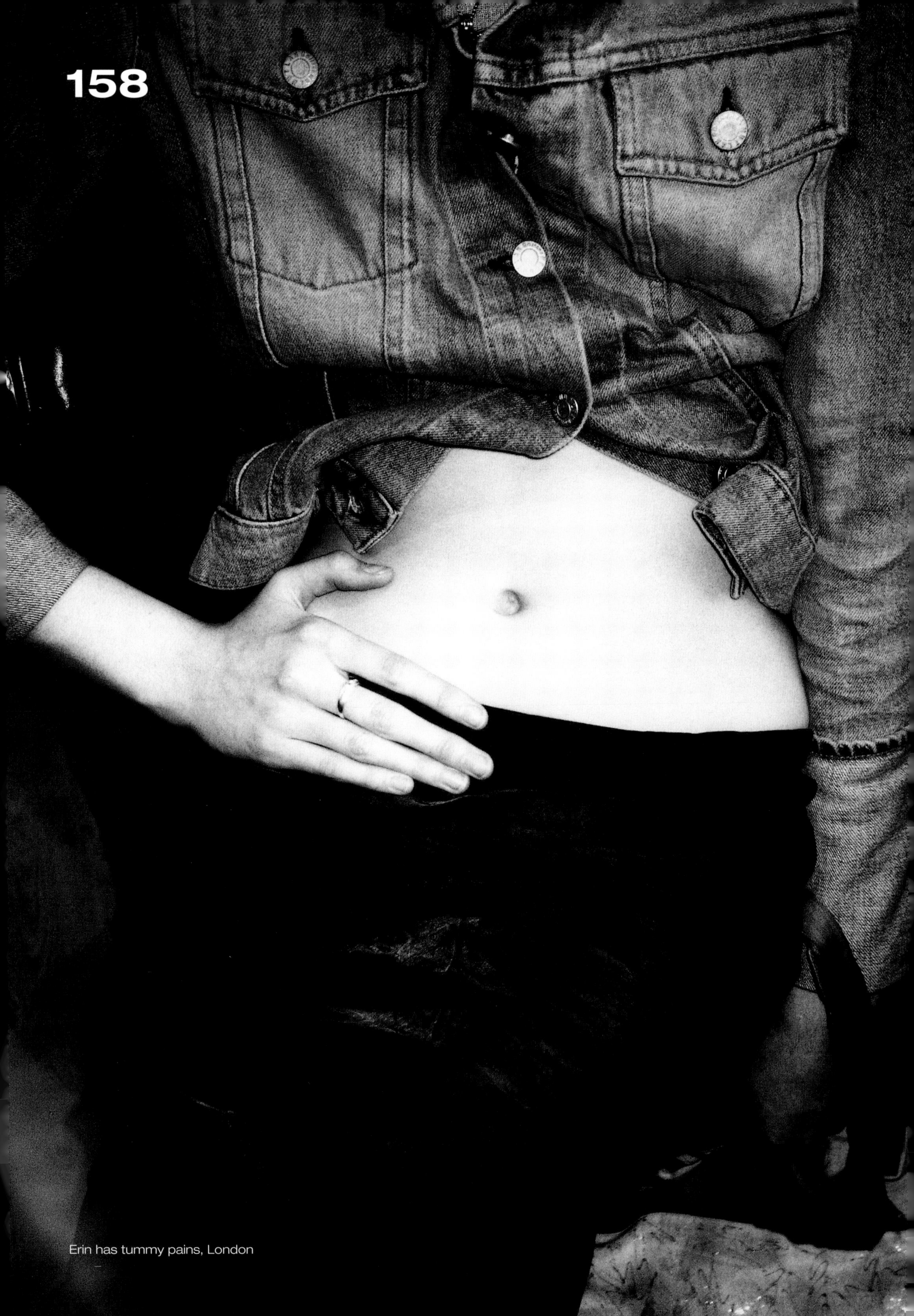

Erin has tummy pains, London

Kubrick and ball, Victoria Park, London

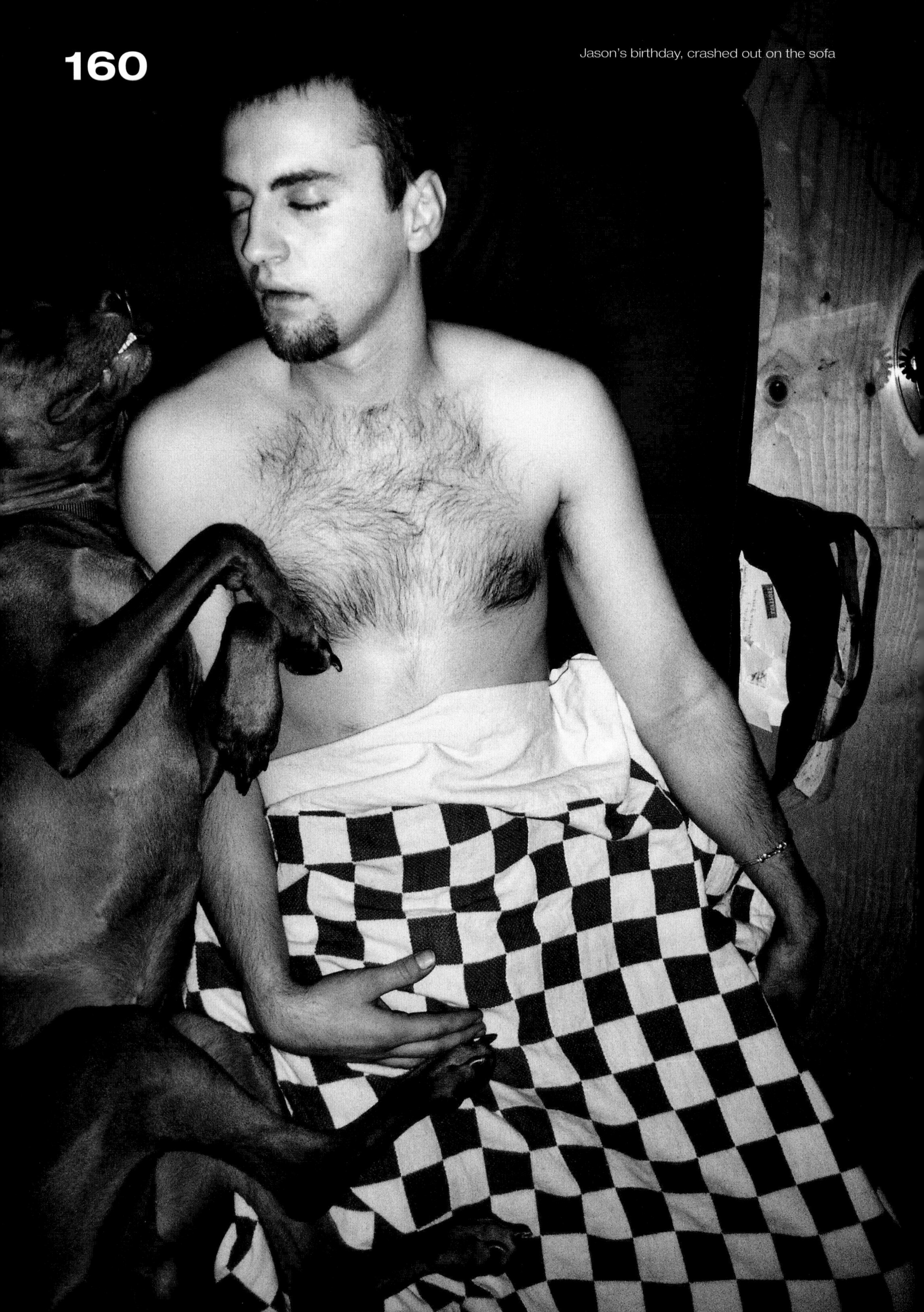

Jason's birthday, crashed out on the sofa

162 Kubrick jumping, Bricklayers Arms, London

163

Fly to Thailand

164–173 A reportage feature on the lives of young Thai boxers commissioned by *Arena Homme Plus*

165

166

TIME

168

169

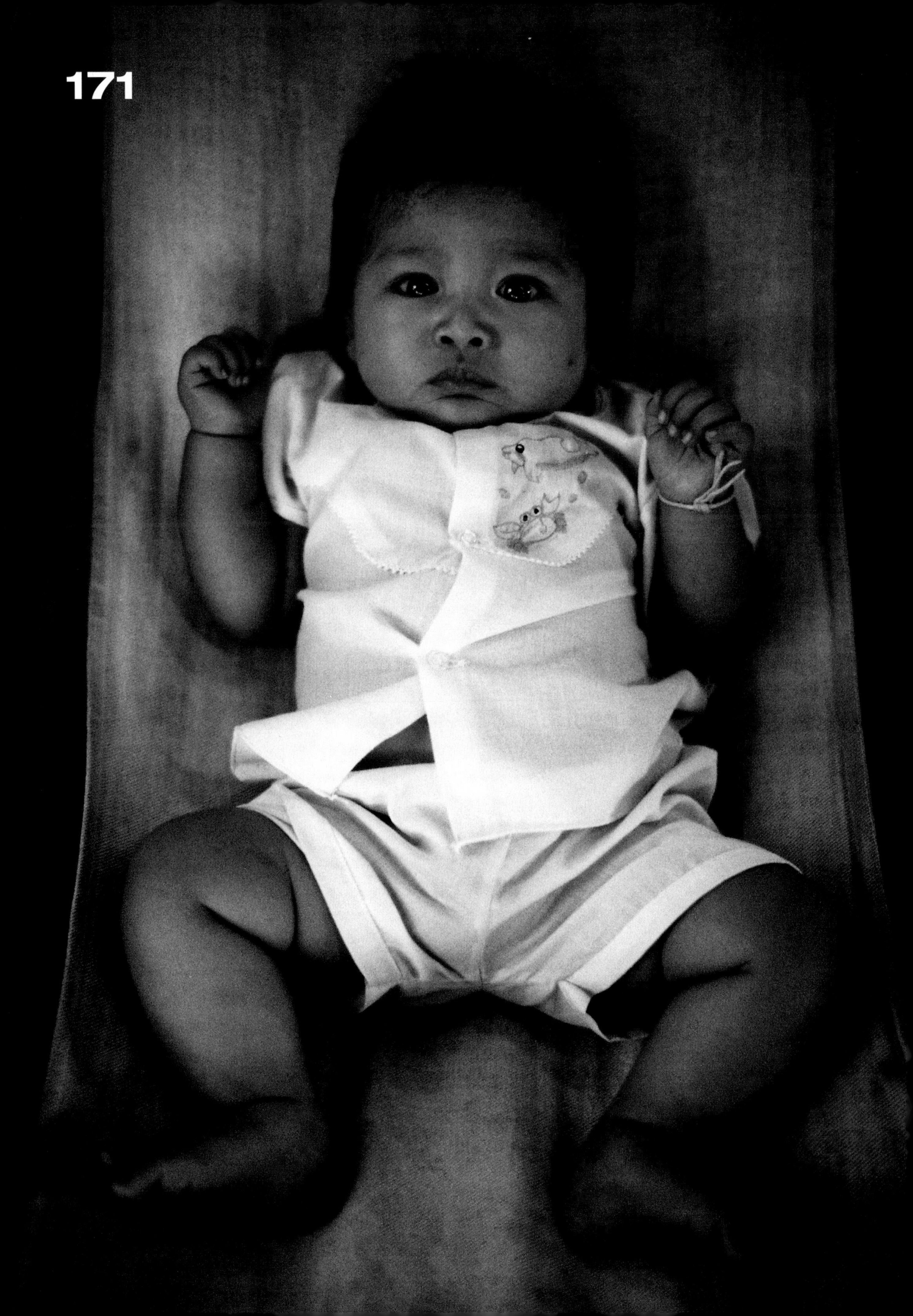

171

elf

174

175  176

177

178

174 Get home and spend the afternoon with Kubrick, Victoria Park, London
175 Fly to New York
176 NYC
177 Street trader, NYC
178 Maggie stretches on the sofa
179 Raphael and Karen kiss on the way to Six Flags, New Jersey
179a The Big Wheel, L–R Raphael, Karen, Jade, Erin and Maggie, Six Flags, New Jersey.

179

179a

180

NYC

181

Cat in NYC

182 A family, NYC
183 Rear window, NYC
184 Erin and me move into a hotel because her apartment is too hot

Karen and Erin join 4th of July celebrations, Times Square, NYC

185

Karen and Erin in a lift for *i-D* magazine

189 View from the hotel window

187 Erin and I have dinner at Lucky Strike, NYC

188 NYC

191

190 A family, Times Square, NYC
191 Erin the night before her surgery
192 I have to fly home
193 The band 'Air' for *i-D* magazine, France

192

193

194 19

194 Paris airport on my return home
195 Ill in bed
196 Treatment for Amanda Ghost promo
197 Erin's surgery scars
198 Erin on the phone
199 Erin and I deal with our spots
200 Erin and Kayte have a beer before we go out, Brighton

197

196

TREATMENT

ARTIST	AMANDA GHOST	TRACK	"FILTHY MIND"
LABEL	WARNER	DIRECTOR	SEAN ELLIS
DATE	17.07.99		

The track is set in a tiled bathroom.

It looks run down and dirty.

The room is lit with a single light bulb that hangs in the middle of the room.

A moth chases the light.

A bath tub sits in the middle of the room and is shielded by a shower curtain.

We see a figure standing in the bath behind the shower curtain.

A cat walks across the floor.

A tap is dripping water in the sink that hangs on the wall. A slow track into the shower curtain.

The curtain pulls back.

The cat hisses.

The tap starts to drip more.

A girl dressed in sexy clothes turns and looks at the camera.

Somebody with no face hits the light.

In the swinging light we continue to montage images.

Writhing bodies, close up of insects, Amanda's performance is intercut with these shots.

She looks sexual aggressive and part of everything that is happening.

A man flies upwards and sticks to the ceiling.

The bath has filled with water and Amanda is in it, her make up starts to run.

At this frenzy point, the ceiling starts to crack and black ink starts to pour in. It covers the light bulb.

It starts to pour through the cracks in the tiles.

Sexy shapes of bodies to get rained on with black ink.

People start to shake.

Amanda starts to shake.

Ink rains down on her as she lip syncs.

People dancing explode in slow motion as ink pours from their bodies.

The sink overflows with ink.

Faces get contorted by forced air.

The swinging light bulb explodes.

END

199

200

Kubrick plays the joker

201

202

202–202a Liisa Winkler for *Numero* magazine

203

Catherine Hurley for *Numero* magazine

203a

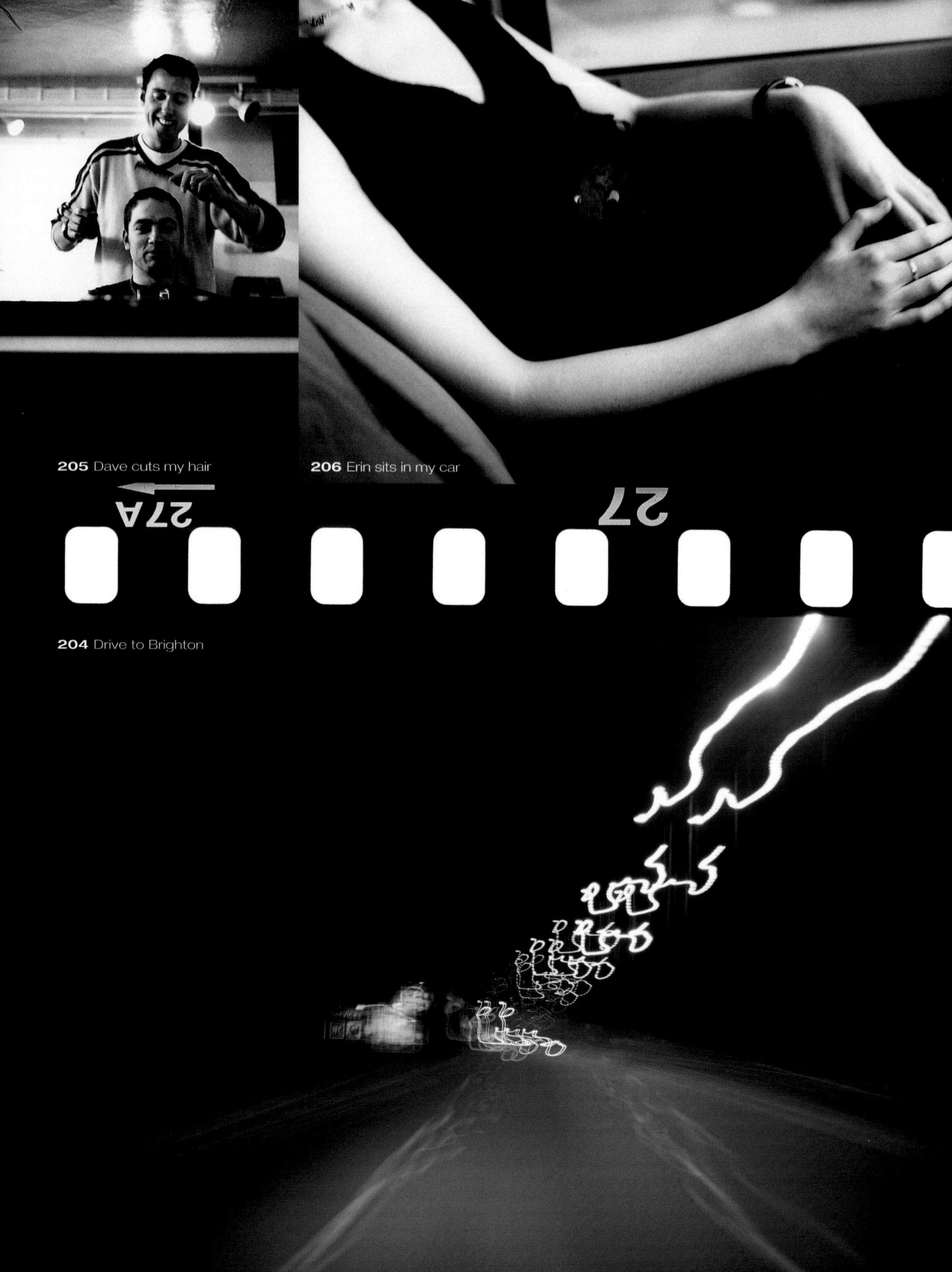

205 Dave cuts my hair

206 Erin sits in my car

204 Drive to Brighton

Eugene Souleiman "The shoot is today!"

208

208–212 Stills from the making of Amanda Ghost's 'Filthy Mind' video

209

210

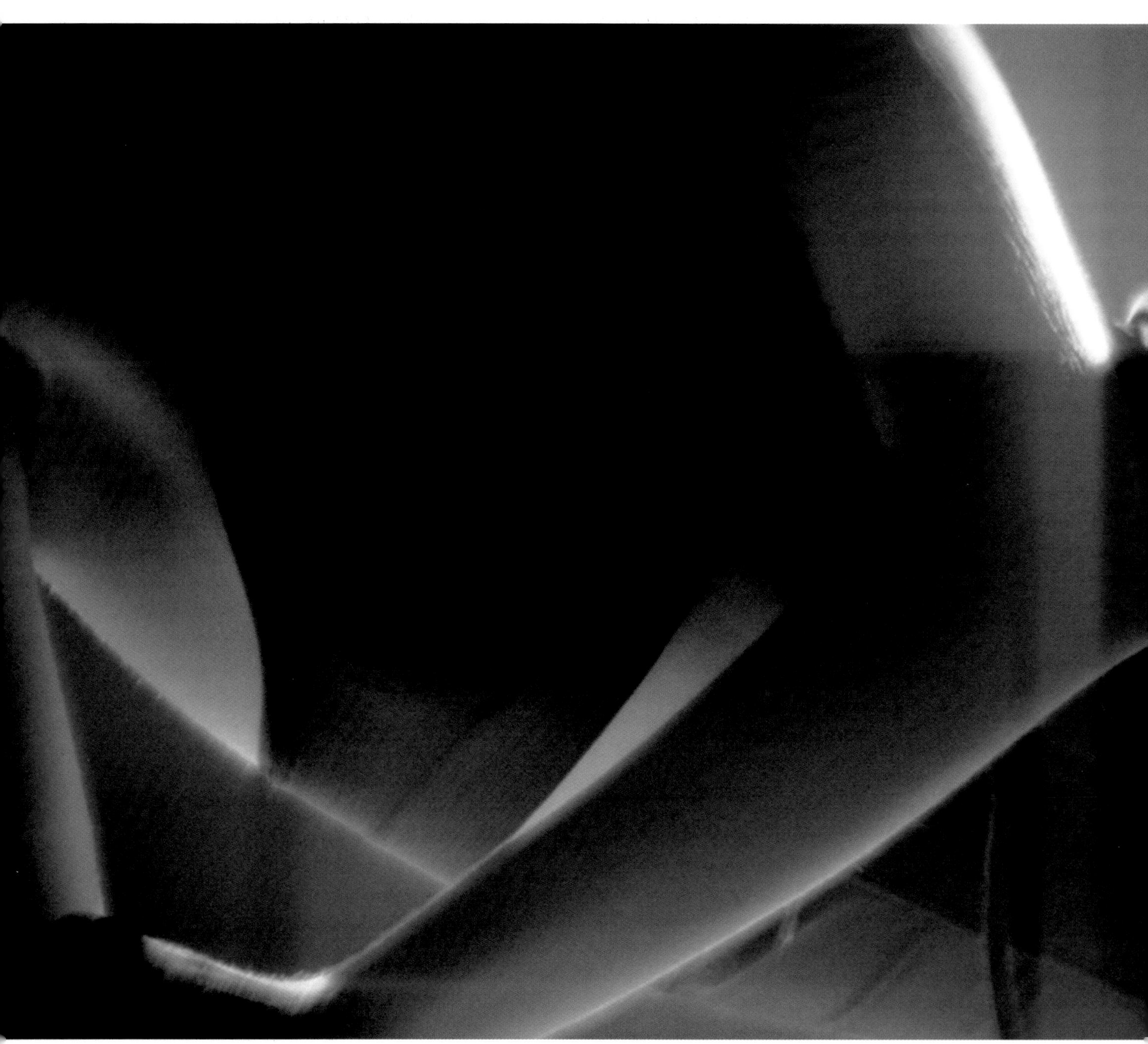

212

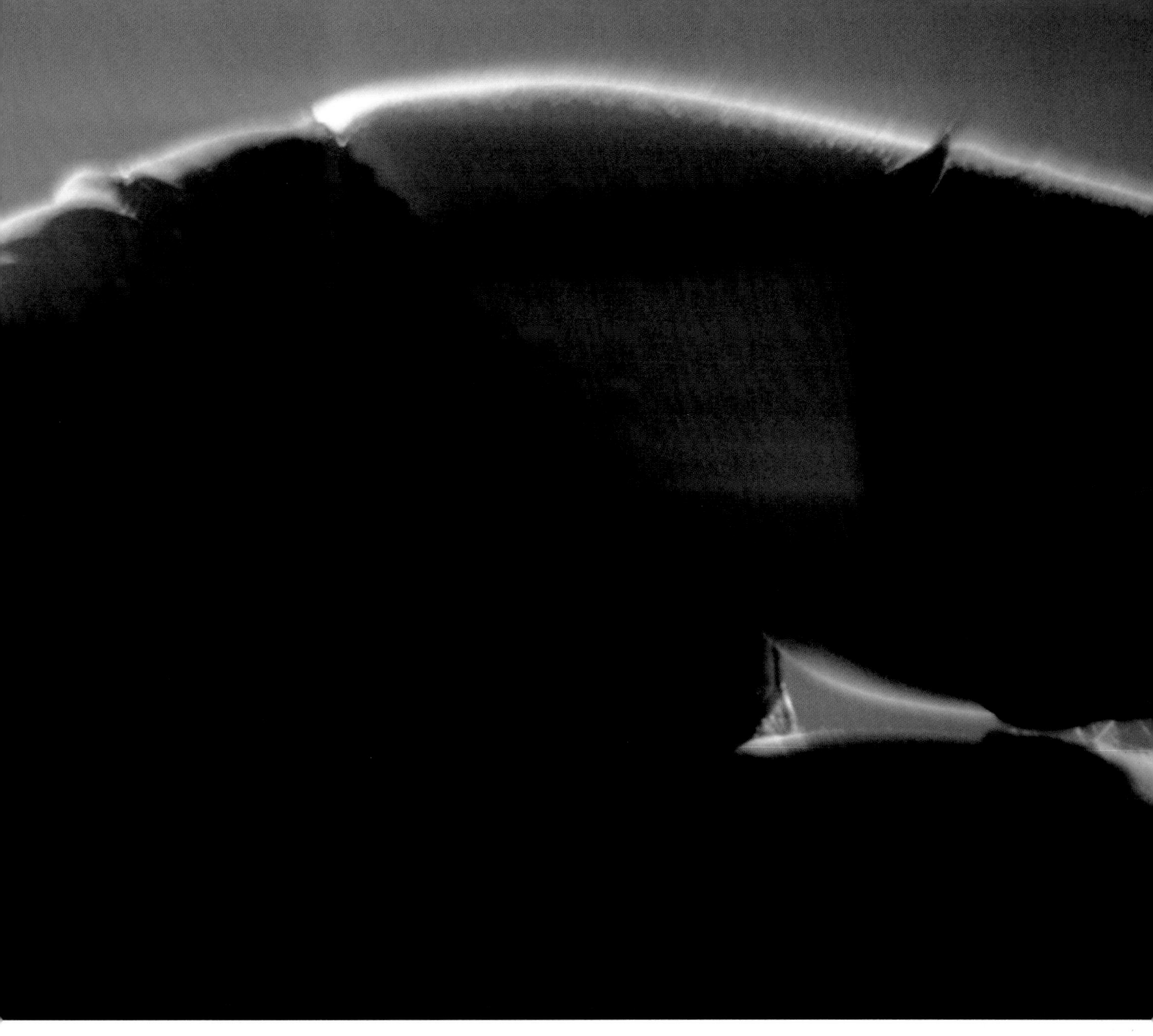

214

213–216 Film stills from the postproduction on Amanda Ghost's 'Filthy Mind' video, London

215

216

217 Fly to Nice with Erin

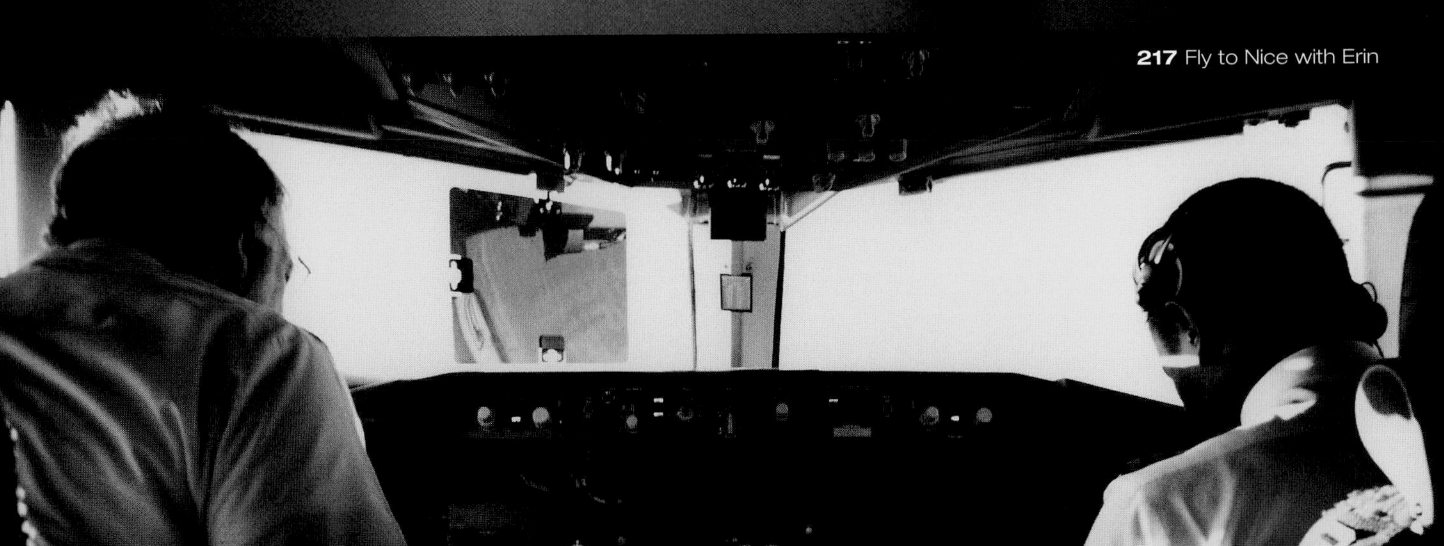

218

Elton John for *Arena Homme Plus*

219 Elton's dog
220 Erin in the hotel lobby
221–222c Postproduction continues on Amanda Ghost's 'Filthy Mind' video, London

221

219
220

224

223 Mum, Dad and Erin watch the solar eclipse, Brighton beach
224 A visit to see my Nan, Brighton
225 Erin and I fly to the Seychelles for a holiday
226 Erin at dinner

227

229

228

230

227 A glass of wine on the beach
228 Giant tortoise
229 Erin and I have a snog in the sea
230 Erin catches a tuna fish on a fishing trip
231 Erin dancing to a CD
232 A young girl who lived near the church
233 Erin in the shower

231  232

234 Erin doing a handstand
235 Gorgeous Erin
236 Erin on a deserted beach

235

236

237

Boys running on the beach

238 Erin at the cashpoint
239 Paradise
241 Towel swans
242 The book I was reading

241

245

244-249 Porn series

246

247

248

249

250

A reprinting of ' A room for an hour' with Mash, originally shot in Tokyo 1998 for *The Face*. Reprinted in London but unpublished

252 **253**

258

252 Kubrick plays with Senna, London
253 Film still from Stanley Kubrick's last film, 'Eyes Wide Shut'
254 Emma on Hampstead Heath
255 Jason in the park
256 Kayte and me aged 3 and 5
256a Kayte and me aged 27 and 29
257 Heather Stohler nude
258 Daphne Guinness

254  **255**

256  **256a**

257

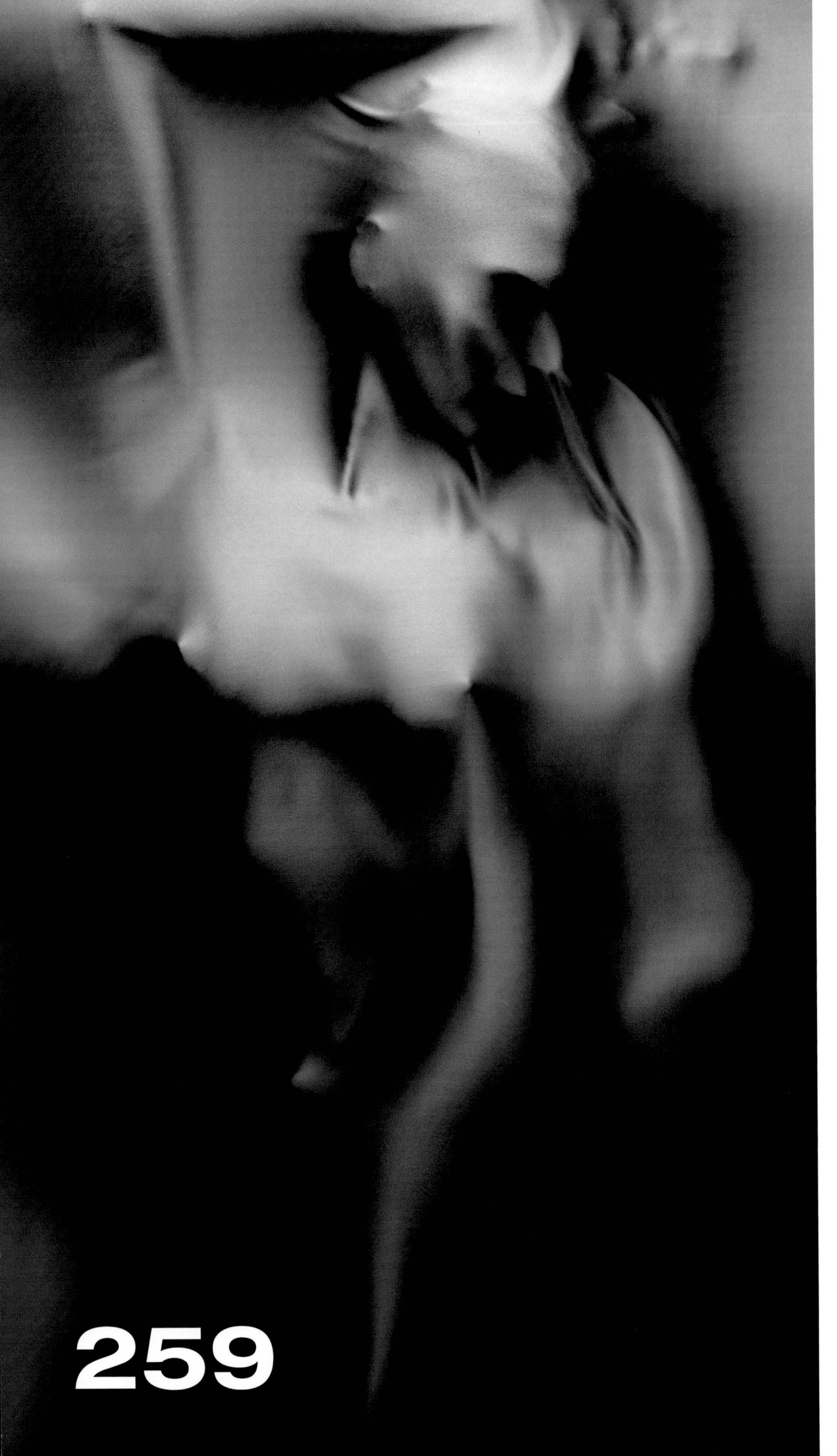
259

Mercury nudes

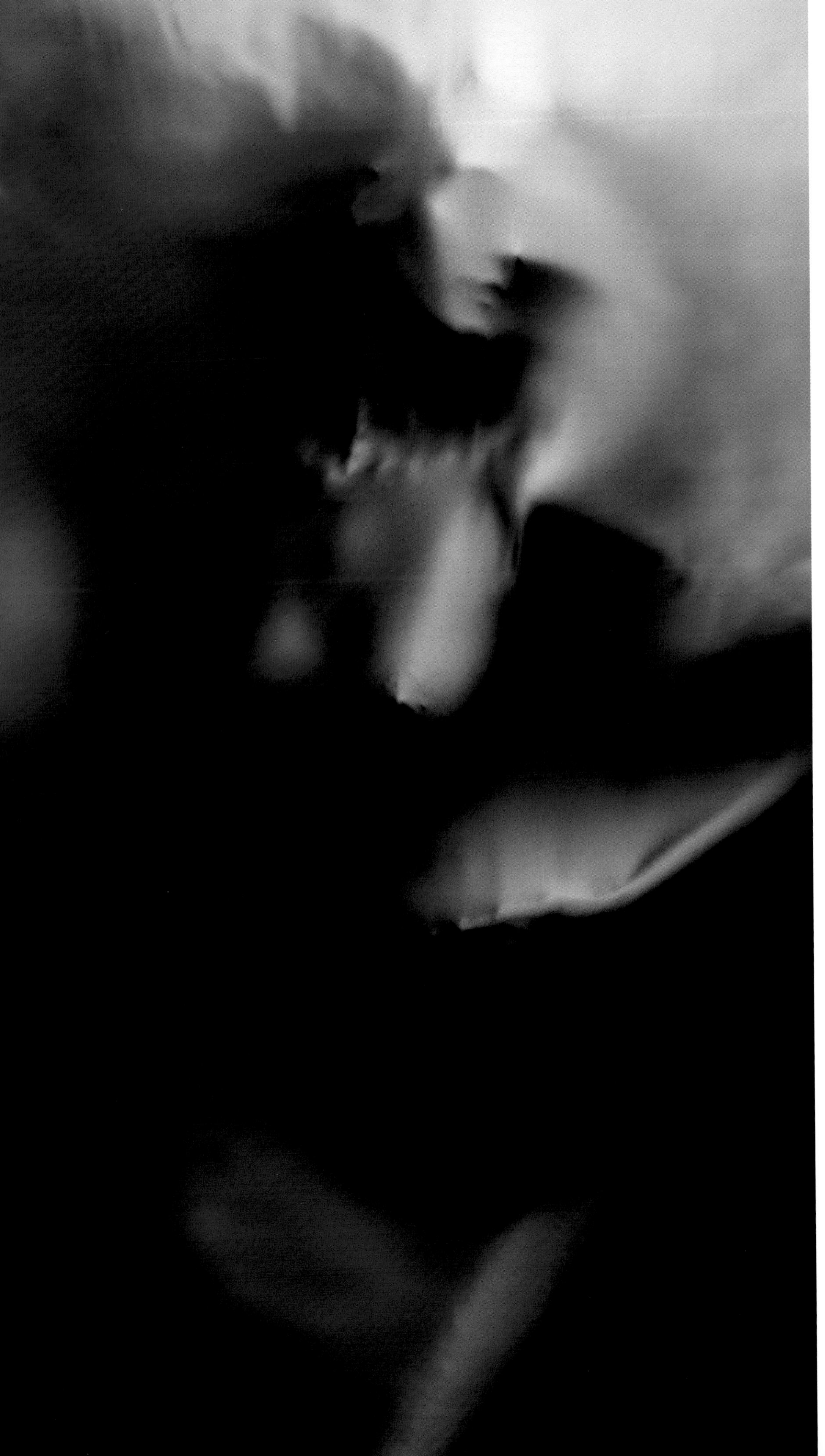

260

261

262

261 Erin and Kayte in a health spa
262 Kubrick in Victoria Park
263 Fashion show, London
264 Natalie and Nicole Appleton
264a Erin picks up Model of the Year Award
264b Rachel Roberts and Vivien Solari

263

264

265 Vivien Solari at Julien McDonald's runway show **265a** Spice Girls watching the show **265b** Julien MacDonald's show **265c** Kate Moss, Julien MacDonald and Mel B **265d** 'Scary Spice'**266** Dinner with Erin

266

267 Erin and Kubrick in bed

268 Matt and Emma

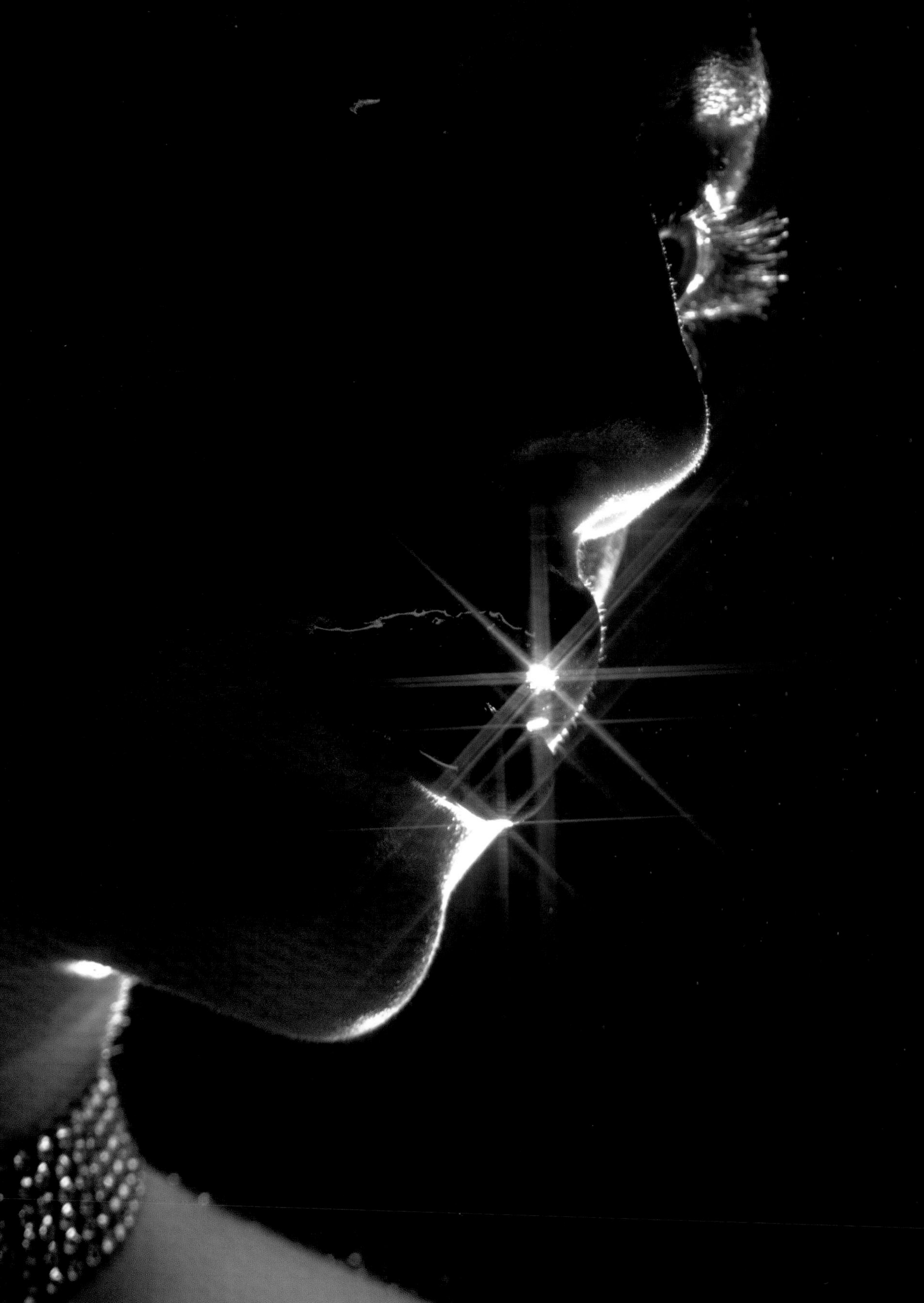

Janelle for the cover of Robbie Williams' single, 'She's the One', London

272

271 Erin in a cathedral, Paris
272 Erin's back, Paris
273 Kubrick and me

273

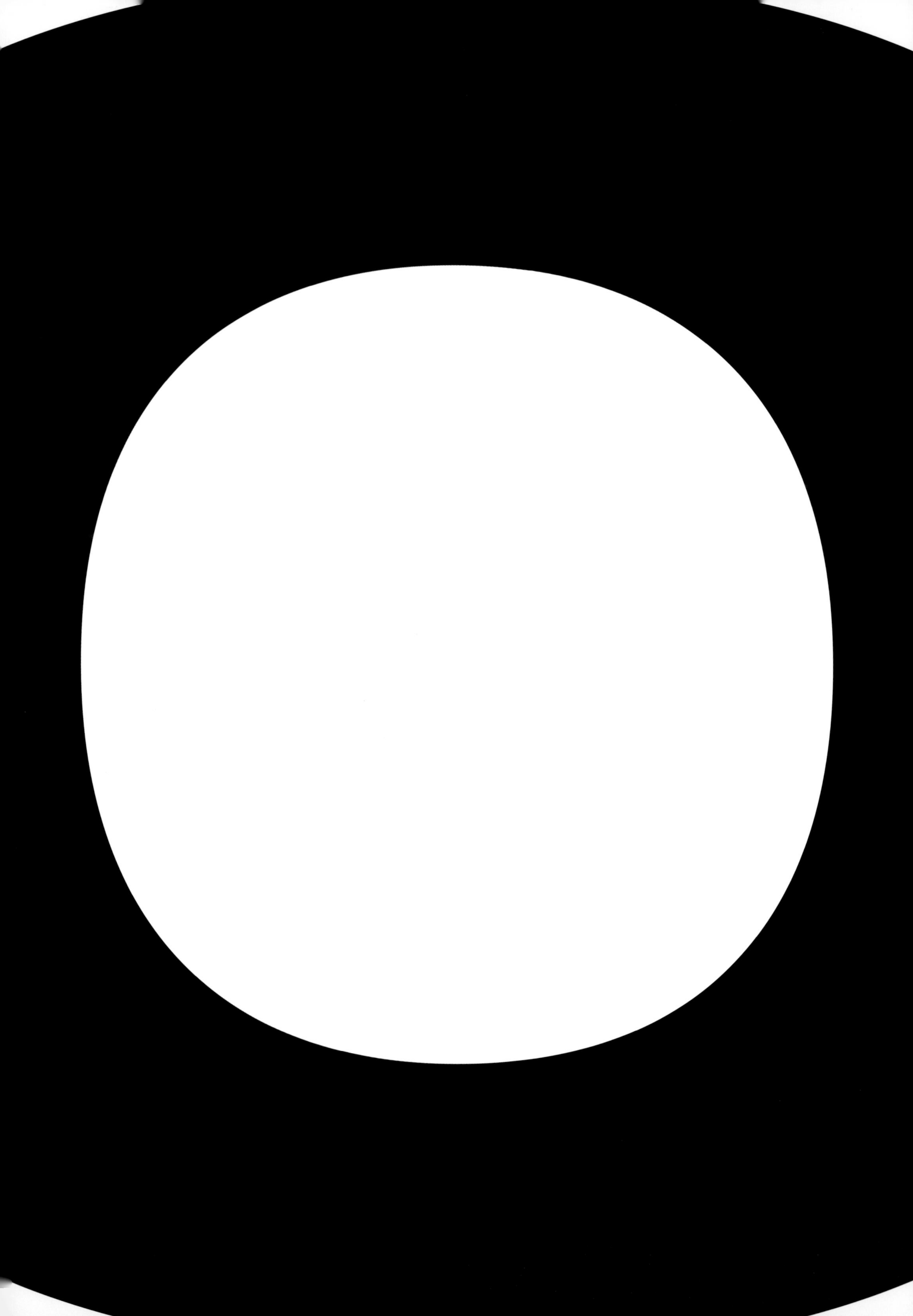

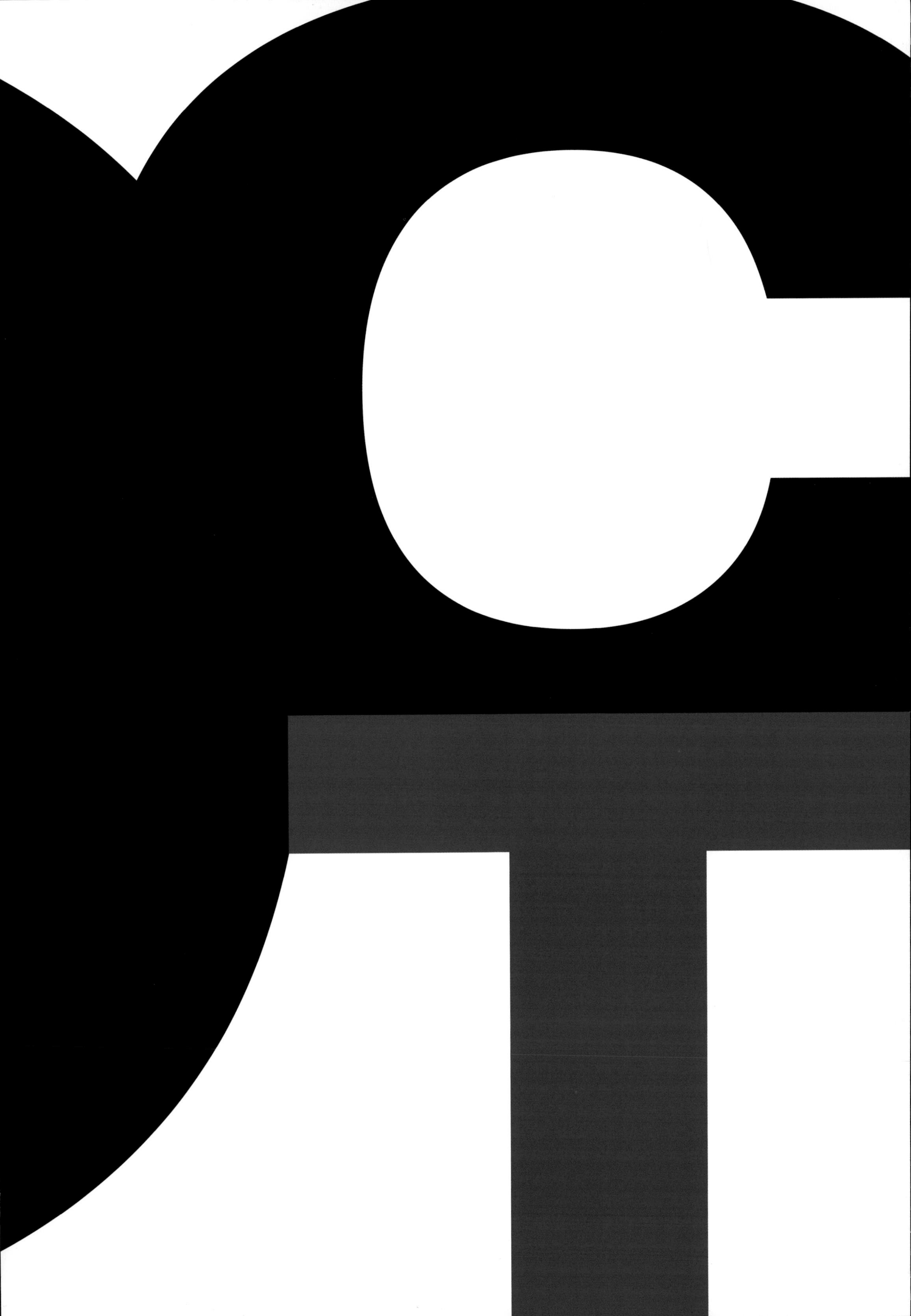

274 Kubrick having fun in the park

275 Neil decides to get pissed

283

284 Sharlene Spiteri and Kubrick pose for some press pictures, London
285 Alex Barber for *i-D* magazine, London

285

284

288

286 Erin fills in a form at the doctors
287 Tabitha Simmons
288 Gio takes a picture of Britney Spears and me at New Orleans airport

287
286

Strip joint, New Orleans

289

290

290 Trent Reznor for *Spin* magazine, New Orleans
291 Fly to New York to pick up Erin so we can fly back to London together

293
294
How to create the perfect man!
Sensitive, Sporty, + big knobbed.
295

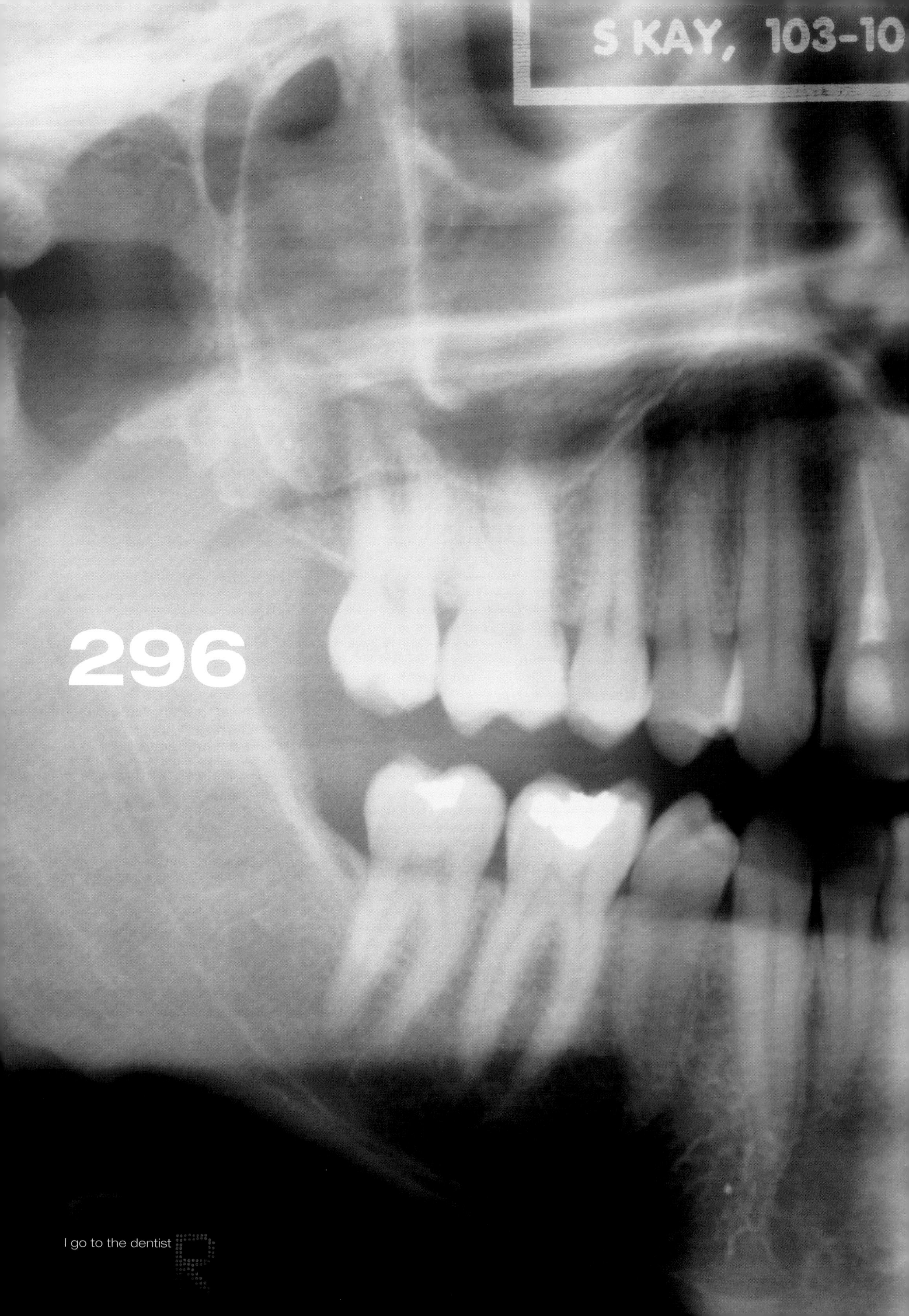

S KAY, 103-10

296

I go to the dentist

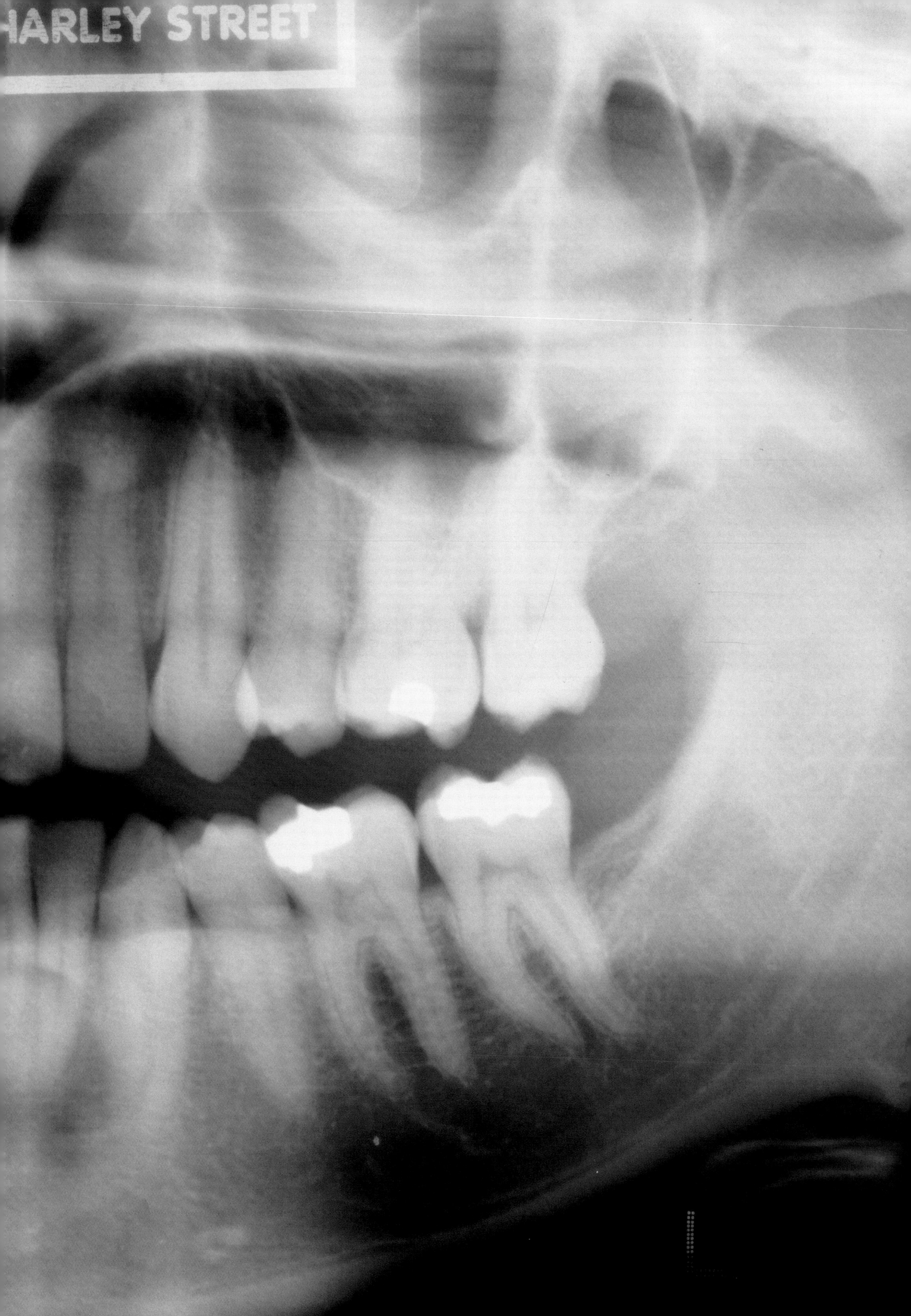
HARLEY STREET

298 Erin on the toilet

299 Swans, Victoria Park, London

297

Kubrick stalks on Hampstead Heath

Two friends get carried away in my flat

301

Nude, London

302 Two Hussein Chalayan fans at a fancy dress party
303 Hampstead Heath, London
304 Rob at a Halloween party

303

304

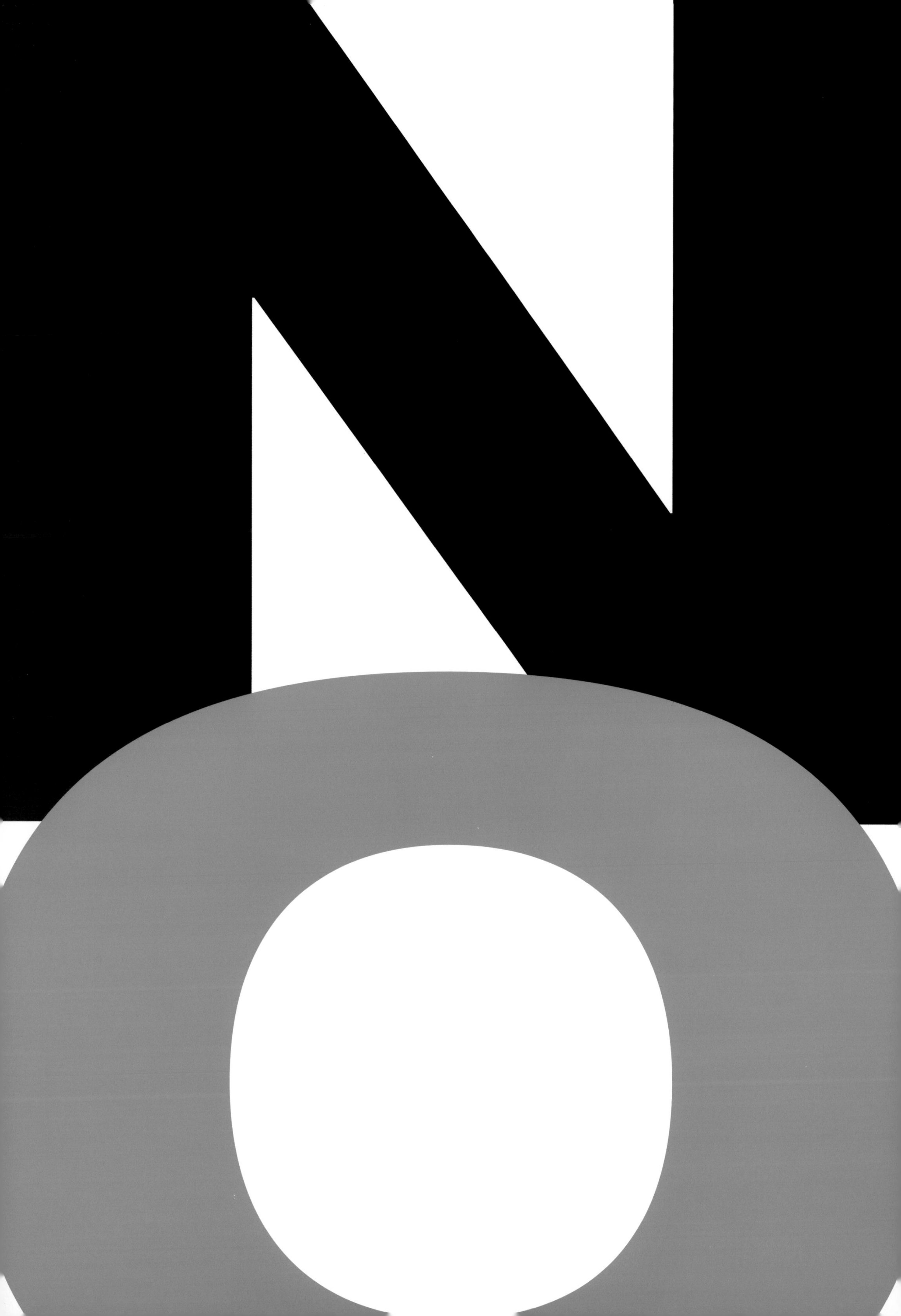

305 Jenelle for *The Face*
306 Sharlene and Matt after Texas play Wembley
307 Morgan Kennedy puts the finishing touches to the Patrick Cox set

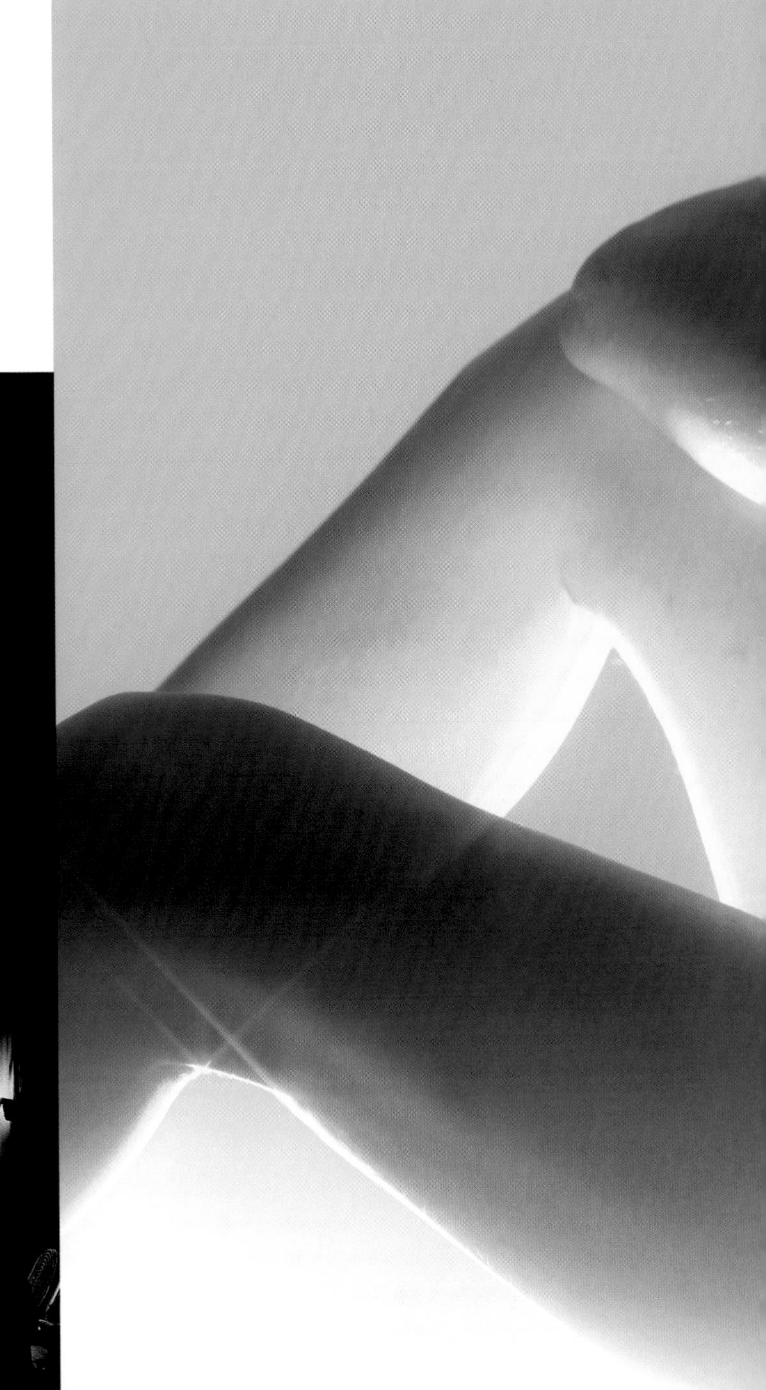

308

Patrick Cox campaign

310

311

312

310 Self-portrait
311 Kubrick jumps for joy
312 Woman asleep on the Eurostar
313 Caroline Ribeiro for a beauty campaign

314 Erin and Kubrick in my office, London

315 Girl smoking

316 Kubrick with stick

317 Kubrick with motorbike

318 Nude

319

319 Rachel Creek on a go-see **320** Eugene and Lisa in the studio, Paris **321–321b** Plein Sud campaign, Paris

320

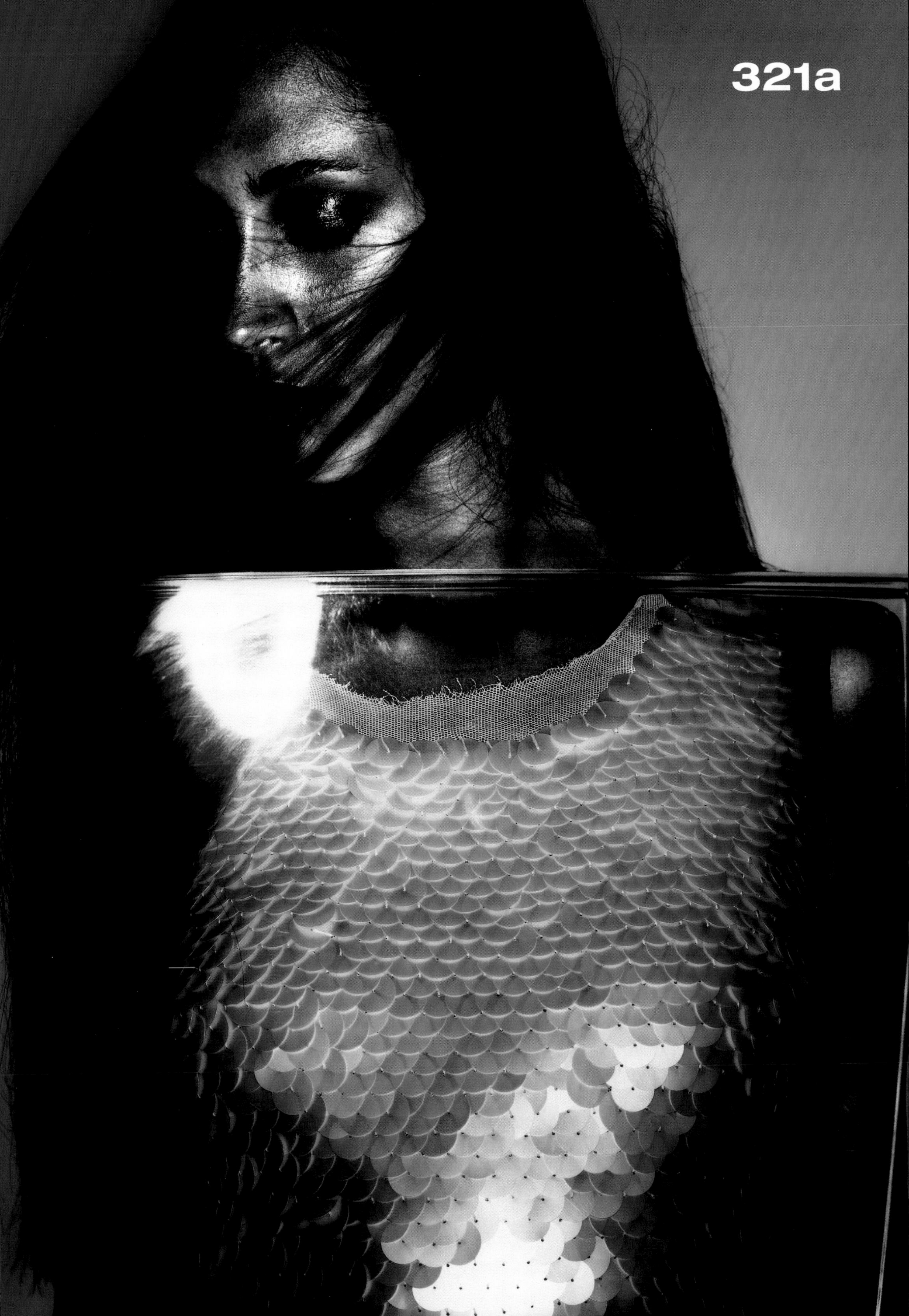
321a

322 Rick Astley and Matt Rice

322a Vanessa Castillejo and friend

322b Ayo, Carla and Antonella

322c Jason and Heather

322d L-R Gillian McVey, Carlo, Kinder, Jeff Lounds and Tim Blanks

323 The Roundhouse, Camden, London

322e Maria Carla and Jason

324 Kubrick in the wind

325 Ana Claudia, Paris

326 I pick up Kubrick from my sister
327 Waiting for black and white prints at Metro Imaging, London
328 My birthday
329 Jason and Kubrick, drunken birthday celebrations
329a Matt Rice passed out
329b Kubrick wants to play pinball
329c Matt Roach wins pinball
329d Erin falls asleep on the couch
330 Epoca with Kirsty Hume

Lisa Butler pregnant with Lyall

Erin outside my flat, London

Viera gets her hair and make-up washed off

333

Jason in a night club, London

334

Kubrick poses for a Christmas photograph

Rachel Creek for *Numero* magazine

336

339

338

337 Rachel Creek for *Numero* magazine
338 Kubrick in Victoria Park, London
339 Nude, London

340

Janelle for *i-D* magazine, St Martins Lane, London

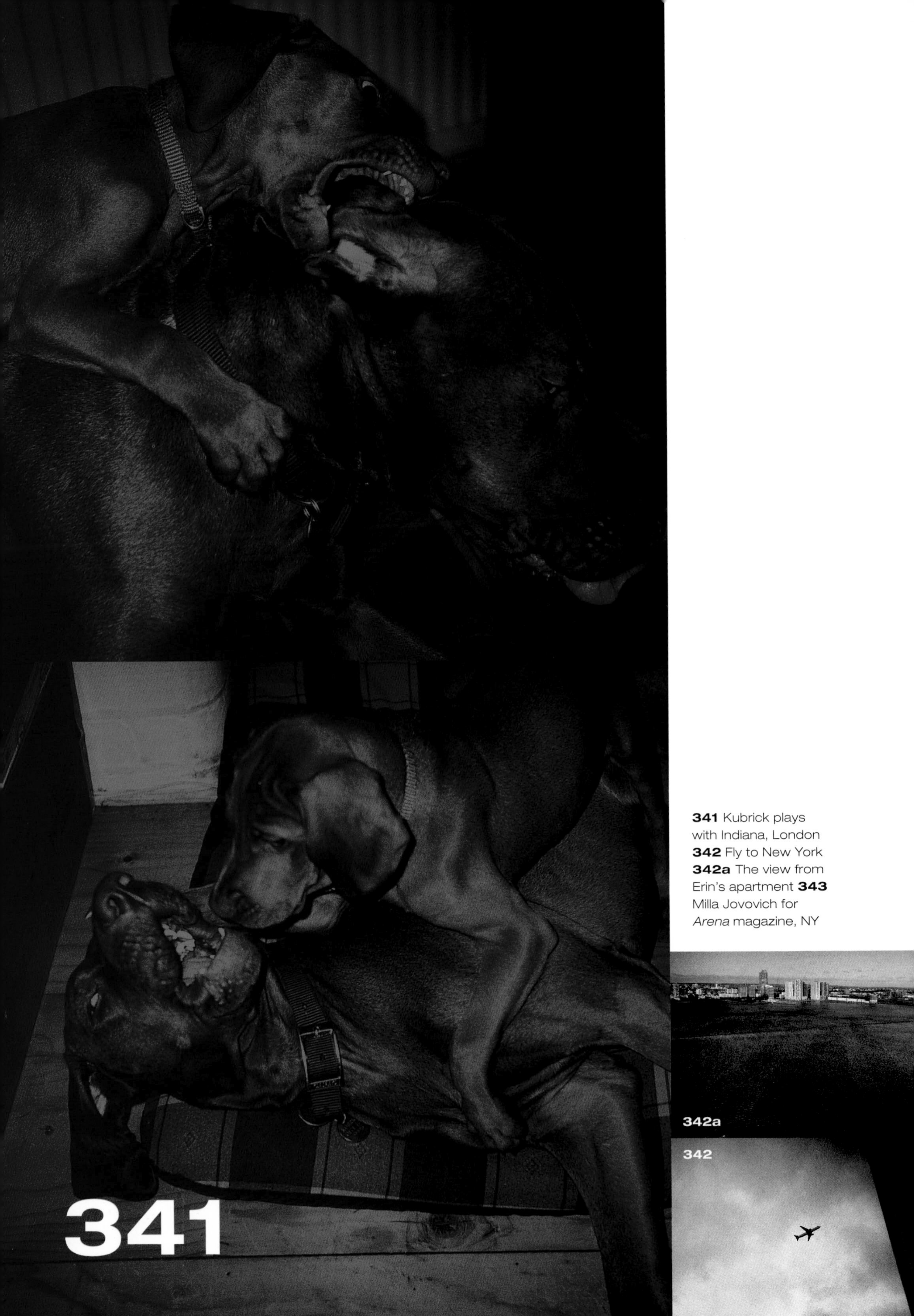

341 Kubrick plays with Indiana, London **342** Fly to New York **342a** The view from Erin's apartment **343** Milla Jovovich for *Arena* magazine, NY

Milla Jovovich for *Arena* magazine, New York

DUCAT

Gisele for Japanese *Vogue*, New York

Heather Stohler for *Numero* magazine, New York

347

Liberty Ross for *Numero* magazine, New York

Liberty Ross in the *Vogue* offices, New York commissioned by *The Face*

349

Heather Stohler in the *Vogue* offices, New York, commissioned by *The Face*

350 Pissed on margaritas, Playa del Carmen, Mexico
351 A walk on the beach
352 Mexican soldiers with puppy
353 "But there are fish in there!" Erin chickens out of swimming in a cenote
354 Fly home for one last job before Christmas
355 Erin in the bath, London

355

353

354

356–357 *Big* magazine,the Horror issue, London

356

357

Erin's Christmas knickers

359 Drive to Birmingham

360 Boxing day at home in Brighton

My Nan and her Christmas decoration

363 363a

362 Drive to Wales
363 Indiana and Kubrick grab a chair
363a Cottage in Wales
364 Matt and Emma's last cigarette
365 Erin and I have a New Year's Eve kiss

364

365

362

365

Last sunset of the millennium

IN LOVING MEMORY OF MY NAN PEGGY PERRIN
1911-2002
&
RAPHAEL DE ROTHSCHILD
1976-2000

Their love of life was a privilege to capture with my time machine.

THANKS TO

To Dad who once told me I was his eyes.
To Mum who has always supported my sister and me by giving us the freedom to explore the world and listen to our findings.
To Erin; my sometimes reluctant model, always in my heart.

To my printers Brain Dowling for his beautiful colour work and Gabby Gassner for her timeless black and white.
To Hank for his endless patience as my Barco artist.
To Matt Rice whose initial first edit helped shape the book.
To Lee Swillingham and Stuart Spalding for their confident and bold design.
With special thanks to Kayte Ellis; my sister and agent.
My assistants Gio and Helen Woods.

And a big thank you to all the people not mentioned who helped fight my corner and made this book possible.